100 Year History of the Gatooma (Kadoma) Library 1917 - 2017

Peter Sternberg & Sheliegh Barton

TSL Publications

First published in Great Britain in 2017
By TSL Publications, Rickmansworth

Copyright © 2017 Peter & Hermoine Sternberg
Photo: Benny Leon
Cover Design: Tamara Sternberg

ISBN / 978-1-911070-99-3

The right of Peter Sternberg & Sheliegh Barton to be identified as the authors of this work has been asserted by the authors in accordance with the UK Copyright, Designs and Patents Act 1988.

All rights reserved. No part of this publication may be reproduced, stored in a retrieval system or transmitted, in any form or by any means without the prior written permission of the publisher, nor be otherwise circulated in any form of binding or cover other than that in which it is published and without a similar condition being imposed on the subsequent buyer.

Contents

Foreword	5
Early Years	7
The Newton Street Library	14
The World War 2 Years	22
On the Move	25
The New Library	33
Exhibition Wing	59
A New Era – Zimbabwe	63
Post Independence	71
The Calm before the Storm	83
The Storm	88
Crisis Time	102
A New Dawn?	111
Anniversaries	113
Chairmen	114
Librarians	115
Acknowledgements	116

FOREWORD

As far back as 1978, when Mrs Betty Conway was approached to write a history of the library, this was a work waiting to be done. The library had a rich history of stories to be told but who would take on this task? It had to be a person deeply committed to the library and one whose very heart lay in all aspects of this amazing complex. No other person could have been more eligible to take on this project than Peter Sternberg. His family had been involved with the library for many years. His father, Robert Sternberg, was the Chairman for thirty years and Peter was Chairman for a continuous period of forty years.

Anyone who has written the history of anything will confirm the hours of research needed to do this job. Peter spent so much time on sorting documents, going through Minutes and reports in order to extract the facts. His aim was to have the booklet ready for the 100th anniversary of the library.

Sadly, this was not to be, as he suffered a massive heart attack and never fully recovered to complete his task. He approached me in late November of 2016 and asked me to assist him with the latter part of this history. I have, of necessity, not had the time to go into the account with as much depth as Peter did, but have completed what he began. Peter Sternberg passed away on the 25th of January 2017. We salute him for his dedication and commitment to the Gatooma/Kadoma Library.

Sheliegh Barton
June 2017

EARLY YEARS

The original settlement of Gatooma, situated in the Midlands of Southern Rhodesia (97 miles from Salisbury and 190 miles from Bulawayo) owes its very existence to the rich gold reefs which were discovered by prospectors and miners in the late 19th/early 20th century and also partially to the fact that the site of the future town lay in the direct path of the national railway line linking Bulawayo to Salisbury, which had been laid in place in 1902.

In 1906 an enterprising agent/trader by the name of Godwin built a couple of huts next to the railway line and established a bush canteen and forwarding agency, from where he supplied both prospectors and newly established mines with general provisions and mining supplies. The name "Gatooma" was derived from a range of low lying hills south of the railway line, known as the Kaduma Hills. Business proved brisk, and by 1907 several commercial buildings had sprung up in this flourishing new settlement. The local mining industry continued to expand rapidly and farms were being established throughout the surrounding district due to the fertile soil found in the area. A post and telegraph office and a police station were provided by the government. That same year Gatooma was constituted a Village Management Board.

By 1912 it was reported that the intellectual side of life in the town was being well catered for by the Gatooma Literary & Debating Society. This organization held fortnightly debates on subjects of immediate general interest to the community, in addition to other topics occurring further afield – for it was mentioned that Gatooma boasted residents of varied experience gained in many parts of the world. These meetings were always well attended and the society, although of comparatively recent growth, had already proved an unqualified success.

Alas, the outbreak of the Great War in 1914 put paid to expansion throughout the country, as many men went off to war to serve the British Empire. Nevertheless, for those remaining at home, life went on as usual, but the limited entertainment facilities available were keenly felt throughout the district, especially by those residing on farms and mines. Readers in the district were fortunate that Gatooma was serviced by a good bookshop, owned by a Mr G. S. Fitt. The bookshop carried a comprehensive range of books, periodicals and newspapers but, unfortunately, not all could afford to purchase these items, virtually all of which were imported, either from South Africa or from overseas. Due to the good service rendered by this bookshop, many local residents had become avid readers over the years, and the need for a library to serve both the budding township and surrounding countryside increased as time went on.

An "embryo" library of sorts was started in 1916 by Mrs Amelia Fitt, the far sighted wife of businessman, George Septimus Fitt, owner of the town's excellent bookshop, when she proposed to the then Village Management Board that a room in their offices be allotted to serve as a small library. This request was agreed upon, and members of this new library were required to donate ten books in lieu of a year's subscription. This venture proved to be highly popular, but as could be expected, soon became severely hampered by lack of space, being confined to a single room, and a small one at that. Membership, it would appear, soon became restricted. Mrs Fitt, incidentally, had started the very first school in Gatooma in 1908 and whilst the village school was still under construction, lions roamed the streets at night. The new school opened in April 1909 and Amelia Fitt took on the position of School Secretary, in addition to being fully involved in running the one-roomed library at the Village Management Board offices.

By 1917, Gatooma had developed into a town, and was awarded Municipal status that same year. The first Mayor to be elected was none other than the previously mentioned George Septimus Fitt, a major supporter of the movement to establish a library in the town. The clamour for a decently sized library had in the meanwhile increased, and so it was that a public meeting of likely subscribers to a library was arranged, and was held in the lounge of Specks Hotel on Friday 30th November 1917. Twenty people turned up, including one lady, and Mr Alex. R. Garrett took the Chair. Mr Garrett and Mr E. R. Blackwell outlined their plans to form a public library, and these were found acceptable. Mr R. W. Pringle proposed that the library be named "The Gatooma & District Public Library" after Mr Calder had suggested that the word "District" be added to the name. Five persons were elected to the first committee, namely Messrs Garrett, Thornton, Pringle, the Revd Green and Miss Phelps. It was also proposed and seconded that Mr E. R. Blackwell be elected Hon. Treasurer. The motion that a room be hired for one pound a month to house the books was carried. And so ended a meeting which would have far ranging consequences over the years to come ...

Directly after the public had left, the new committee sat down and drew up the new rules. Subscriptions were set at 2/6 per month or an annual fee of 25/-, plus an initial entrance fee of 10/-. Subscribers were allowed to take out two books at a time and library hours were set from 6-7 p.m. on Mondays, Wednesdays and Saturdays. Books could be kept for 14 days at a time. A banking account was opened with the Gatooma branch of the Standard Bank (an account, incidentally, that was until recently, still in use). Mr Garrett was elected Chairman of the library and Mr Thornton elected Vice-Chairman, with the Mayor and Deputy Mayor elected Trustees.

By the end of December 1917 the sum of sixteen pounds had been collected in subscriptions plus deposits from 37 aspiring new members.

The first committee meeting of 1918 was held at the Mines Office on Friday 11 January and a number of accounts were tabled for payment, including the sum of one pound, being in lieu of monthly rent, due to the landlord, Mr G. S. Fitt, for the new library was housed in a room situated behind Fitt Building, which was situated in Rhodes Street – the first two storey building constructed in Gatooma. Apart from discussing a quotation received for insuring the books, no other business as such was discussed.

No trace of further committee meetings was to be found in the very first Minute Book until one recorded on Monday, 2 December 1918, which meeting took place at the Mines Office. It was noted that the Annual General Meeting was to be held on 5 December 1918, three days hence. Under an item headed "Accommodation" the Hon. Treasurer mentioned that there was no room left in the library to affix further shelving for additional books. It was agreed that this problem should be dealt with by the new committee due to be elected at the forthcoming AGM.

The First Annual General Meeting was held in the lounge of Specks Hotel on Thursday 5 December 1918 at 5 p.m. It was proposed and seconded that the entire committee be re-elected en bloc, which was carried unanimously and a hearty vote of thanks was proposed to the outgoing committee. It was noted that there was a possibility that the books belonging to the Cam & Motor Mine Library (Eiffel Flats) might soon be available for purchase. The Hon. Librarian, Mr Blackwell advised the committee that he was departing on six months' leave, and a member of the committee, Mr Thornton, was appointed to act in his place.

At a subsequent committee meeting held on the 21st March 1919, members were informed that the premises next door to A. A. Searle had been offered by the owner, H. W. Campion, to the library at a monthly rental of five pounds. These were obviously larger premises, and it was suggested that the library combine with the trustees of the mineral exhibit on display as far as the front shop was concerned, the idea being to have a combined reading room and geological exhibition open to the public. It was likewise suggested that a suitable public war memorial for the recently ended 1914-1918 World War be constructed in the form of a building housing both the library and the geological museum. The Librarian was presented quotations on new books from a London firm of booksellers, Messrs Simpkin, Marshall, Hamilton, Kent & Co., and was instructed to purchase books from this firm in the future.

During the course of the year it would appear that Mr Blackwell, the original Librarian, failed to take up his position again following his six month period of leave, for at a committee meeting held in March 1920, acting Librarian Mr Thornton was granted an honorarium of five guineas.

At the 1921 Annual General Meeting it was decided that subscriptions be raised to 15/- (fifteen shillings per quarter), 25/- half-yearly and 50/- per annum. At this meeting Mr Thornton tendered his resignation as Librarian and suggested "that the present automatic system by which readers take and return books be terminated and some system under the supervision of a paid assistant should be adopted at the earliest possible moment".

A permanent Librarian's position was advertised and four applications were received, including one from "Anonymous". The post was offered to a Mrs A. E. Smith who took on the title of Librarian/Secretary at an annual salary of £40. Mr Thornton was appointed Honorary Librarian for past services rendered. The library hours of opening were now fixed as 4.30-5.30 p.m. on Wednesdays and Fridays and 11.00 a.m.-1.00 p.m. on Saturdays.

However, by the end of the year problems had arisen. Chairman Garrett explained at a General Meeting that although subscriptions had been raised, the library's position had not improved and there appeared to be no chance of obtaining new books, on account of which membership had dropped. Not less than £50 per annum was required for the purchase of new books, but with rent alone amounting to £80 per year, and the Librarian's wages amounting to £40 per year, plus a drop in membership, there seemed to be little possibility of attracting more members to join the library.

It was suggested that a dance should be held in order to raise funds. Library membership fees were reduced to 10/- quarterly, 17/6 half-yearly and 30/- yearly in order to both retain current members and hopefully attract new readers. It was also proposed that a small overdraft be procured from the bank in order to purchase some sorely needed books. It was also agreed to try and sell some 300-400 of the current book stock and the Secretary was asked to write to Sinoia (a small town north of Salisbury) where there was a new farmers hall being opened, and offer the books to them.

In January 1922 the Librarian announced her resignation and new applications were called for. It was also discovered that the annual rental payable amounted to £60 and not £80 as mentioned at the previously held General Meeting. The Chairman also announced that overdraft facilities amounting to £25 had been authorized by the bank to enable new books to be purchased and £5 was immediately allocated for this purpose. It was agreed that new book titles acquired by the library be advertised on a regular basis in the *Gatooma Mail*, a local weekly newspaper (and this would continue over the next 80 or so years).

Three applications for the Librarian's post were received, from which Mrs A. F. Clark was chosen, commencing her duties on February 1 1922 at a salary of £3 per month, plus an allowance of 5/- for a black African assistant.

A committee was formed to organize the fund-raising dance which took place in May and £17.12s.6d worth of tickets were sold. After deducting £8.7s.0d for expenses, a nett sum of £9.5s.6d was raised for the purchase of much needed books. It is noted that 25 books were ordered from Darter Bros. in Cape Town early in 1923 and books were regularly ordered directly from Britain to supplement local purchases.

At the Annual General Meeting held in April 1923 it was revealed that after a stock take of books, there turned out to be a shortage of some 388 novels plus 43 works of travel etc. valued at 2/6 each. It was agreed to write these missing books off as there appeared no way in which they could be traced. It was emphasised that these losses had occurred prior to the current Librarian having commenced her duties. The stock take had shown that the library now possessed some

1,400 works of fiction, 270 books on travel and 37 reference books; a total of 1,707 books in all. The library appeared to be making good progress, for there were now 47 subscribers, the highest number achieved so far. With almost 200 books having been acquired during 1922, additional shelving space had once again became a priority. Once more the call for the building of a library was raised. In September 1923 the good news was received that the government had decided to provide the library with a grant amounting to £66 for the year in question.

At the AGM in January 1924, it was announced that the government had donated Stand No. 42 in Newton Street for the purposes of building a library, on the condition that a building valued at not less than £500 be erected within a period of two years. The Chairman was once more re-elected, and other matters decided during the course of the year allowed casual members of the library to take out two library books at a time at the cost of a "tickey" (three pence) per book, plus an initial deposit of 10/-. It was also agreed to now pay the black African cleaner the sum of 7/6 per month. Unfortunately, bad news was received in August of the year when the government informed the Chairman that they had decided to cancel their offer of Stand 42 to the library.

In September 1924, Mr Garrett resigned as Chairman and likewise from the committee, (but re-joined the library committee in 1930). In his place, committee member Lieut-Colonel J. A. Smith (a local farmer) was elected Chairman of the library. The committee now consisted of 10 members, which included Mrs G. S. (Amelia) Fitt, who had become a devoted and tireless worker for the library. Apart from books purchased from local suppliers, second-hand books were now being purchased on a regular basis from the Times Book Club, £2 per month securing a total of four books. To bolster funds, such suggestions as the holding of crossword competitions, bridge drives, concerts and dances were put forward. Subsequently, a crossword competition was held which resulted in a nett loss of £3.3s.6d.

During 1925 no less than 72 new novels were purchased from the Times Book Club, thus greatly boosting the fiction section. In May, the Gatooma Municipality paid a grant of £21, and in November 1925 the government paid the library an annual grant of £52.10s.0d. The reading room at the time stocked the following newspapers: *Rhodesian Advertiser, Livingstone Mail, The Gatooma Mail, Rhodesian Opinion* and the *South African Mining & Engineering Journal.* In addition, one kind member (Mrs L. Brooks) regularly donated magazines such as *Punch*, *The Bystander* and *Wide World Magazine* for the table in the reading room.

The position regarding the much needed new library resurfaced once again and it was proposed that a letter be written to the Colonial Secretary requesting the offer of a stand. It was also proposed that requests for donations be sent to Colonel du Pont, Sir Ernest Montague and Mr Abe Bailey (the Rand mining magnate, who, it was rumoured, had acquired over a million acres of land around Gatooma).

At the Annual General Meeting held on January 29th, 1926, it was reported that membership stood at 30 paid up members plus a further 10 members who had to date not yet paid their dues. During the previous year, five new members had joined and 11 had resigned, of which eight had left the district. The Chairman, Lieut-Colonel Smith, sent in a letter of resignation, and in his place, Dr S. A. Clark (husband of Mrs Clark, the Librarian) was elected Chairman of the library for 1926.

THE NEWTON STREET LIBRARY

Early in 1926, the government notified the library that it had decided to renew its previous offer regarding Stand 42 Newton Street, providing certain conditions were met. Amongst these conditions was the stipulation that the library committee appoint Joint-Trustees to the Board, and these two trustees were to be the Civil Commissioner (Mr Francis Joseph Clarke) and the Mayor of Gatooma, who happened at the time to be Mr George Septimus Fitt. The news caused a surge of optimism throughout the community, and the Gatooma Town Council decided to increase its annual grant to £31.10s.0d, with the proviso that the public reading room would stock the *Rhodesia Herald*, *Bulawayo Chronicle* and *Gatooma Mail* on a permanent basis.

Library Chairman, Dr Alan Clark, set about designing plans for the long awaited library building and in due course tenders were submitted from a number of local builders. A number of tenders were received, of which the highest sum quoted amounted to £936 and the lowest £750. It was agreed to go ahead with the construction of the building and a loan of £630 was obtained from the Gatooma Hospital Trustees in April 1926 at an interest rate of seven per cent, the capital to be repaid within 10 years from date of occupation. A separate library building account was established with the local branch of the Standard Bank. The contract to construct the actual building was awarded to Mr A. de B. Spurr.

It would appear that many of the materials used in the construction of the building were ordered by the library directly and supplied to the builder, as 30,000 bricks were ordered from Mr C. Crowther at a cost of £2.12s.6d per 1,000. Materials were ordered and tenders awarded to firms and individuals based almost exclusively in Gatooma:- Mr Marneweck supplied river sand, A. J. McIntosh & Co. tendered £16.15s.0d for gutters, down piping and flashing. Mr I. Rosenberg painted the library and supplied glazing for the sum of £30, and other firms and individuals including R. W. Taylor (an early pioneer), Johnson & Fletcher Ltd and Colin John Campbell (who, 34 years later, was to have the town's prestigious new Theatre Complex named after him), supplied large quantities of building material.

Presumably, the new library was completed towards the end of 1926 or possibly early in 1927 – for at the October 1926 committee meeting it was proposed that notice be given to Mr Campion, landlord of the premises in which the current library was housed, that his premises would soon be vacated. Minutes of that period make no mention of a date as to when the new library was actually opened, or for that matter, whether any ceremony was held to mark the occasion, but it can be assumed that by early 1927 the library had moved into its own premises. The important factor was that the library was finally housed in a building specifically designed to serve as a library, and that space to house sufficient shelves and increasing book numbers (to commence with anyway) was not at a premium. As from date of occupation, as had been agreed, the sum of £5.12s.9d began to be paid on a monthly basis to the Gatooma Hospital Board in repayment (capital and interest) on the loan secured for the construction of the new library in Newton Street.

NEWTON STREET LIBRARY COMPLETED CIRCA 1928

Dr Clark declined re-election as Chairman at the 1928 AGM, citing that he would be away a great deal during the course of the year, and proposed that Eric Fitt, son of George Septimus Fitt and his wife Amelia should take on the position of Chairman for the ensuing year. This proposal was unanimously carried. Eric Fitt, born in 1899, joined the newly formed Royal Air Force during the latter stages of World War I, serving overseas, and later made history by becoming the first Rhodesian born Mayor of a Rhodesian town (Gatooma), a position he held for several years. Eric Fitt was to serve as Chairman of the Gatooma Library for a continuous period of 12 years (1928-1939) and one final time in 1954.

During the year, debate was given to the advisability of leaving newspapers and periodicals in the unlocked public reading room, available for members and passers-by to make use of, for there appeared to be a fair amount of theft of reading material taking place. A notice, offering a reward of £2 to anyone supplying information of persons removing these items, was placed in the reading room. The black African cleaner employed by the library was now also tasked to keep an eye on the reading room at regular intervals (shades of 70 years later)!! Two comfortable cushioned Morris chairs were added to the reading room furniture, and good use of the reading room continued to be made by members and non-members alike. A subscription to the popular *Sunday Times* newspaper (Johannesburg) had been taken out, and members regularly donated their read copies of the *Manchester Guardian*, *Daily Sketch* and *John O'London* amongst others. It should be noted that several local newspapers were subscribed to such as the *Rhodesia Herald* and the *Bulawayo Chronicle*, and that virtually all these newspapers were donated by their publishers, a philanthropic gesture that, over the years, gradually fell away! By the end of 1928 membership of the library stood at 55, a net increase of 12 over the previous year.

Membership of the committee was enlarged to 12 in 1929, and Eric Fitt was re-elected Chairman and it was noted that former Chairman. Lieutenant-Colonel Smith re-joined the committee. Mr Colin John Campbell attended the AGM as the Gatooma Town Council representative. Mrs Amelia Fitt proved to be, as always, a very active committee member, and was elected to serve as the Honorary Secretary and Treasurer of the library, and a special vote of thanks was given to Mrs Clarke, the Librarian, on her efficient running of the library.

An advertisement to recruit new members was screened for a month at the local "bioscope" (the town's only cinema – the Royalty Theatre). The library committee also decided that a major fund raising project should be undertaken in order to obtain a matching grant on a pound for pound basis from the Beit Trust, a major Rhodesian charitable organization. In October of that year a dance was held, which proved successful, and netted a profit of £18. Funds were elicited from firms, organizations and individuals. The small

Gatooma Amateur Dramatic Society for one donated five guineas (five pounds and five shillings), and further monies were raised at every opportunity. By the end of 1929 the sum raised had already amounted to no less than £177. No mean feat.

At the 1930 Annual General Meeting, Mr Eric Fitt was re-elected Chairman, and Mr A. R. Garrett, the first Chairman of the library, re-joined the committee. At this meeting, Mr Colin John Campbell was profusely thanked by those present for his splendid effort in raising the sum of £230 for the Beit Trust Fund scheme. In July 1930 the Beit Trust paid the library their agreed share of £158.10s.0d and with much relief, the entire loan of £630 was repaid to the Gatooma Hospital Trustees within a period of only four years (instead of the negotiated 10 year period).

Although the residents of Gatooma were served well by the library, there were many country residents who, despite being avid readers, found it difficult to venture into town and join the library. Life on distantly placed farms and mines must have been very lonely at times, there being no radio, no daily newspapers, primitive road conditions, seasonal flooded rivers, few telephones and often no electricity connections, plus other factors. The library committee debated the matter and agreed to assist by instituting a new category of membership – the Country Member. Secure zinc boxes were purchased from Mr A. J. McIntosh for the sum of £1 each, which included a padlock and these were placed into service.

Eight books at a time were packed into this metal box and were taken down to the railway station, where they were placed into a guards van of a goods train by the staff of Rhodesia Railways (or transported by the R. R. Road Motor Service) to their destination. Boxes were regularly delivered to such sidings or villages as Umsweswe, Battlefields, Hartley, Gadzema, Makwiro, Golden Valley and Chakari, and even as far afield as Wedza and Karoi. Instituted during 1930, the Country Membership scheme proved very popular and was supplemented by book post when a special postal rate for library books came into being. The metal box service as such was withdrawn by the latter part of the 1950s, and had served its purpose very well.

An arrangement was reached with British South Africa Police (BSAP) Mess in the town that, for a total annual subscription of £3, membership would be granted to all members of the police force residing in the Gatooma Police Mess (quarters), a gesture greatly appreciated by the police. A complete 32 volume set of the *British*

Encyclopaedia, including a bookcase wherein to house them, was presented to the library by Dr Coke, a former resident of the town. Mrs G. S. (Amelia) Fitt was made an Honorary Life Member in recognition of all the work she had done since the inception of the library

In August 1930 the Librarian, Mrs Clark, was granted leave of absence due to ill-health, and Mrs Joan Fitt (wife of current Chairman Eric Fitt) agreed to stand in until her return.

It was pointed out at the 1931 Annual General Meeting that membership had unfortunately decreased (the depression appeared to be taking effect) and compared to the previous year's figures, subscriptions had fallen by £23. This, in actual fact, meant a loss of £46 pounds to the library's overall finances as the Government Grant was given on a POUND for POUND basis. Economy measures were placed into operation, and it was decided to cut off the supply of electric light during the summer months at the library. New book purchases from now were to be limited to a monthly total of £6.

On Thursday April 21, 1932 no quorum was obtained at the monthly committee meeting, only the Chairman, Mr Eric Fitt, committee member Mr H. Burrows and the Secretary Mrs Amelia Fitt braving the weather as a severe tropical thunderstorm had descended over the town, turning many roads into quagmires, and worse. It was with a heavy heart that the Chairman officially reported the death of Mrs S. A. Clark, the Librarian, who had passed away after a long illness. Mrs Clark's initiative, energy and enthusiasm had kept the library going during difficult times and she had been largely responsible for its growth and development. Her loss, he stated, would be greatly felt.

At the May 1932 committee meeting Mrs Joan Fitt, the Chairman's wife, who had filled in the post of Acting Librarian during the late Mrs Clark's illness, was elected to the post of Librarian.

By mid-1932 it was found that space was becoming limited in both the lending section and the reading room, and discussion centred on possible additions to the building. It was also noted, and with some relief, that the Government Grant recently received amounted to £64.2s.6d which equalled the previous year's figure, for it had been feared that this grant would be cut, in line with the general drive to economize throughout the country.

At the AGM held in March 1933 it was reported that membership had risen to 63, which number included eight country members serviced by the zinc box/railway route. Appreciation was extended to the lady members of the committee who met regularly to repair damaged books. Mr Campbell pointed out that he travelled regularly throughout the Colony and made a point of visiting libraries in other towns: his feelings were that the Gatooma Library compared most favourably with any of those in other centres.

A sign of the times – later in the year it was proposed that 269 selected books be presented to the M'Tao Forestry Station for use by the men in the Unemployment Camp (1933 being at the height of the worldwide depression which had affected Rhodesia badly), and this offer was gratefully accepted. The committee decided to proceed with the extensions to the library after receiving confirmation from the Beit Trust that they would donate up to £110 on a POUND for POUND basis. Four local contractors submitted quotations and Mr A. Green's tender, amounting to £188 was accepted. (For the record, the most expensive tender submitted amounted to £336).

The extensions to the library were speedily finalised and on Saturday morning 27 January 1934 an "Open Day" for the public to view the newly enlarged library was arranged – teas being provided "on the house" to all those attending. Library committee member Mr Phil Levy, owner of the town's well known Specks Hotel, very kindly provided tables and china (crockery) for the event, staged in order to attract new members to join the library. Some 185 catalogues of books stocked by the library were printed at a cost of 1/4d each for this event, and these catalogues were sold both to members of the library and to prospective members at price of 1/6d per copy.

Insurance on the building and contents was increased to a value of £1,650. New book acquisitions were regularly advertised, free of charge, by the owner and publisher of the weekly *Gatooma Mail* newspaper, Mr Joe Burke. During the year, books were re-classified under the Dewey Decimal System, and in addition to the 13 newspapers and periodicals still being donated by the publishers, the library also subscribed to other newspapers, which included the weekly edition of the *Cape Times*. A total of eight periodicals were being subscribed to, which included *Good Housekeeping* and *Popular Mechanics*. Readers were certainly well catered for. So well, in fact, that the committee agreed to keep the public reading room open in the evenings, and it was arranged for the Specks Hotel night porter to walk up to the library each evening and lock up at closing time, this being 10.00 p.m.

Mrs Joan Fitt resigned from her Librarian's post in September 1934 and re-joined the committee. Appointed in her place was Mrs G. S.

(Amelia) Fitt. The library proved as popular as ever. At the beginning of 1935 it was announced that membership had increased to no less than a 100, of whom 15 were country members. Unfortunately, mutilation and theft of periodicals from the reading room reared its ugly head and, in mid-1935, the decision was reluctantly taken to close the reading room at the same time as the main library, this being at 6.00 p.m. 1936 proved likewise to be a steady year for the library; by the end of the year membership had risen to 123, including 30 country members. Boxes of books for country members were sent far and wide and destinations included Shamva, a small farming village situated no less than 176 miles from Gatooma! In February 1937 an Honorary Life Subscription was bestowed upon Mr Godwin, a true pioneer and founder of the town, who, in 1906, had built a hut for himself right alongside the railway line, and proceeded to open up in business as a forwarding agent, serving the early mines in the surrounding area. Later in the year, a clock was purchased for the library in memory of the late Mrs A. S. Clark, and to this day is still on display in the new library building, together with the original plaque attached next to a photograph of the late Librarian who had served the library so well.

**TOP: CLOCK WITH PLAQUE
RIGHT: MRS A.S. CLARK**

The Librarian had been requested during the year by a number of members to consider purchasing two stamp catalogues to be placed in the reference section. This request was turned down unanimously by the committee as they considered these books not suitable for a public library. The reason given was that "the people who took them out would need them so much and keep them for such a length of time that it would be difficult to keep control of them". Whether they were referring to the people or the catalogues is not mentioned, but there were obviously no philatelists amongst members of the library committee at that time! However, reason seems to have prevailed when, two months later, the committee reversed their decision after having received a number of letters providing good reasons why stamp catalogues should be purchased.

The 21st Annual General Meeting of the library was held in February 1938 and Mr Eric Fitt gave a brief resume of the history of the library. Despite his protestations, which were ignored, he was elected Chairman for the eleventh successive year!

The Librarian/Secretary, Mrs G. S. (Amelia) Fitt (the Chairman's mother), fell ill and passed away in April 1938. Her wonderful work and personality had made the library what it was and she had devoted a great deal of her time to the efficient running of that institution. She would be greatly missed. Mrs Phyllis Dixon, a committee member since 1929, who had proved a tireless worker for the good of the library, was appointed Librarian in Mrs Fitt's place.

The 1938/39 rainy season proved to be a heavy one and it was found necessary to install additional down pipes, as the overflowing storm water from the roof had considerably dampened the walls of the building. Apart from the committee members, no subscribers bothered to attend the 1939 Annual General Meeting and it was concluded that members must be satisfied with the library service and facilities as they had not taken the trouble to attend! Subscriptions to a number of reading room magazines were terminated and these magazines were replaced by *The Tatler, Aeroplane* and *Time & Tide*. And with the repeated thefts of newspapers (which occurred mainly on weekends) rearing its ugly head again, the reading room hours on a Sunday were restricted to between the hours of 10.00 a.m. to 12.00 noon, with the black African assistant on duty to keep a watchful eye on readers! In July, as a mark of appreciation, an Honorary Life Membership was bestowed upon Chairman Eric Fitt for his unstinting work on behalf the library.

In August the Librarian received a letter from country member C. A. Smith informing her of the fact that his home had burnt down and with it the box of library books that had recently been forwarded to him. In view of the fact that the books were old, he was requested to pay only one guinea (one pound and one shilling) in compensation, despite that this sum did not fully cover the cost of the books which had been destroyed.

Due to popular demand, the library facilities already allowed to members of the BSA Police stationed in Gatooma were now extended to men stationed in Norton, Battlefields and Chakari. This was duly noted in an issue of the BSA Police magazine *The Outpost*.

THE WORLD WAR II YEARS

After a continuous period of twelve years in the Chair, Eric Fitt stood down at the 1940 Annual General Meeting. He was succeeded by Mr Phil Levy, who was elected in his place. It was noted that since the outbreak of war some months earlier, regular supplies of periodicals from the United Kingdom were being disrupted (probably due to enemy action), and that the price of books had risen. Reading room opening hours were extended and the public could now enjoy its facilities from 10 a.m. to 6 p.m.

The August 1940 monthly committee meeting was attended only by the Chairman, Mr Phil Levy and three ladies as the "gentlemen members" were all unable to attend due to the fact that they were undergoing war time training in the town. It was then decided to hold the committee meetings at 6 p.m. on the second Tuesday in the month after drill parade was over. In November 1940 the Librarian, Mrs P. Dixon, tendered her resignation as most of her time was taken up by war work. Mrs E. M. Davies assumed the duty of Librarian/Secretary on the 17th December 1940.

At the 1941 Annual General Meeting Mr Levy stepped down as Chairman and Mr Fenton was elected to the post. Due to the shortage of new books caused by the war, the Librarian was instructed to release books immediately they were received from booksellers, and that this should hold good until the end of the war. It was further agreed that some of the older periodicals be donated for the use of troops stationed in Southern Rhodesia. Books and periodicals were also sent to members of the police force who were at the time guarding bridges in the Hartley (later renamed Chegutu) area. Books were now being sourced from bookshops in Salisbury, as it was presumed that book orders from the London bookshops had been unattended to due to the blitz.

An enquiry was made whether members of the Indian community were allowed in the reading room. It was decided that, as ratepayers, they had every right to make use of the reading room facilities.

The lawn and garden being somewhat run down, it was decided to approach the Civil Commissioner and request the use of black African convicts to work in the garden. It was also suggested that a somewhat "better class" of black African employee be engaged and that he be paid an increased wage of £1.15s.0d a month in addition to "skoff" (food rations). A member of the library residing in the township of Eiffel Flats (some four miles from Gatooma, site of the Cam & Motor Gold Mine) offered 11 volumes of *Punch* magazine to the library for the total sum of £6 as her son had gone off to war, but this offer was declined by the committee.

The Annual General Meeting, held on 11 March 1942 saw Mr Fenton resign as Chairman due to his transfer from Gatooma. Mr P. Levy was voted into the Chair. The Librarian, in her annual report, mentioned that the blitz over London had devastated the book trade and that Simpkin & Marshall of London, where the library had obtained the majority of their books, had lost over four million books alone in the bombings. Paper shortages were also in effect. Despite these problems, some 346 new books had been purchased during the 1942 year and membership stood at 111. Total books in stock now amounted to approximately 7,250.

During the year, the popular South African magazine *The Outspan* joined the periodicals available in the reading room. It was agreed that surplus reading material be donated to the Internment Camp housing some 1,500 Italian civilian male internees from former Italian colonies in East Africa (Abyssinia and Somaliland). This camp was situated some five miles from Gatooma on the Bulawayo Road. (In later years this camp became the nucleus for the Ngezi Township). On a point of interest, the monthly electricity and water account paid to the Gatooma Municipality averaged £1.15s.0d per month during 1942. In future years the library would not be levied on the consumption of water by the municipality which was a great help.

The 1943 Annual General Meeting, due to be held on March 8th was aborted due to the fact that virtually no one attended, thus no quorum was obtained. The meeting was rescheduled to March 30th, and Mr Phil Levy was re-elected to the Chair. He presented a very satisfactory report for the year, which was well received. Annual membership subscriptions were increased to £2, but it was decided that clergymen throughout the district should be exempted from paying membership subscription – a move much appreciated by the gentlemen in question. A selection of additional magazines was subscribed to which included *National Geographic*, *Life*, *Time* and

Readers Digest, all of which were to prove very popular with readers over the years to come.

The 1944 AGM saw Mr Levy step down and Mr J. M. (Jim) Wixley elected Chairman for the ensuing year. In November of that year Mrs Bell (committee member) and Mrs Phelps were thanked for the donation of children's books to the library. This appeared to be the very first time that children had ever been considered as making use of the Gatooma Library – and proved to be a major breakthrough, for no mention of a children's section, or even of children for that matter, had ever appeared in any previous Library Minute Book!

1945 saw Mr Wixley re-elected Chairman, and the Librarian reported that membership had increased and once again more books had been purchased than in the previous year. It was noted that the reading room stocked no less than 26 different newspapers and periodicals – a remarkable number by any standards. A proposal was put forward that the children's section should be developed, as the current selection of books was somewhat old and found to be inadequate in numbers. The committee agreed to look into this. It should be mentioned that any children who made use of this embryo "children's section" required parents who were library members, and a child was permitted to take out just one book at a time. No additional fees were levied for this facility – however, the child's book was included as being part of their parent's allocation of books.

In March 1945, Past Chairman Phil Levy suggested that an entirely new library should be built. The following month the committee agreed to write to the Southern Rhodesian State Lotteries for possible financial aid for a new library building. Later in the month the junior section was boosted when a whole selection of new books, obtained from bookshops in both Salisbury and Bulawayo were received by the library, and parents were notified accordingly. In September it was unanimously agreed that the Librarian's salary be increased to £10 per month – and that this increase be retrospective to January 1945. Mr Levy tendered his resignation from the committee in October 1945, for he had recently sold Specks Hotel and had decided to leave Gatooma in order to retire. He was sincerely thanked for his past services to the library.

ON THE MOVE

Mr John Bertram Hodges took over the position of Chairman in 1946. In July of that year Mrs Edith Davies tendered her resignation as Librarian, as she was moving to Salisbury. Seven applications for her post were received and Mrs McIlleron was selected to take her place. It was agreed by the committee that for the remainder of the year no more than five new children's books be purchased each month.

The present library building was found to be in sore need of repair and a local builder suggested that buttresses be built to supplement the east wall. It was pointed out however that this might not turn out to be a permanent repair, as the whole of the lean-to addition to the building was found to be faulty in construction. Some of the walls had cracked, and water had leaked into the library. Likewise, water appeared to be seeping under the foundations.

BUTTRESSES BUILT TO PROP UP LIBRARY WALLS

To round off the year, the black African employee was awarded a 5/- "Xmas Box" (bonus) and it was decided to increase his monthly wages from £1.7s.6d to £1.10s.0d as from the first of January.

Mr John Hodges was re-elected Chairman for 1947, and informed those present at the Annual General Meeting that the committee was seriously considering building a completely new library, and that the Rhodesian State Lotteries was prepared to provide a grant of £1,000 towards the scheme. He also stated that the children's section had added 89 new books to its shelves during the previous year, and that this had proved a most popular move with the young readers.

It was agreed that the reading room would be closed on 10 April 1947, this being the occasion of the Royal Visit to Gatooma of King George VI, Queen Elizabeth and the two Princesses, Elizabeth and Margaret, who were due to arrive that day on the Royal Train. During their brief stopover at the railway station, the Royal Family were introduced to the Mayor and Mayoress, Councillors and their wives plus various dignitaries, and half of Gatooma's residents were expected to gather at the station to celebrate a "red letter day" which would always be remembered by all those present.

In July the Gatooma Municipal Council offered a vacant stand, situated in the new Civic Centre, for the purpose of housing the proposed new library complex. The laws stated that, as the present library stood on ground which had been donated by the government, such ground could not be sold by the library committee. Shortly thereafter a letter was received from the Town Planning Department in Salisbury, informing the committee that the title to the current piece of ground in use (Stand 42), free from any restrictions, could be purchased from the government for a sum based on its current municipal valuation. It was unanimously agreed to purchase the Stand (land only) for the sum of £552; that being its municipal valuation.

The junior section of the library received a boost in November 1947 when it was agreed that children could become members of the library in their own right upon payment of an annual subscription of 2/6 plus an additional 10/- deposit. Parents of Junior Members could revert to taking out their original four book allocation and Junior Members could choose books from the junior section. Originally, children whose parents were not members of the library were barred from joining, but this ruling was now cancelled, and children could become members whether their parents belonged to the library or not. This proved to be a great step forward for the youngsters of the town and encouraged children to join the library.

It was pointed out to the committee in a letter by the Town Planning Department that the library was not in possession of a proper constitution. An up-to-date and proper constitution was soon drawn up to rectify this overlooked matter. Sixteen local organizations were approached with a view to raising funds for the proposed new library complex, in which it was hoped to house a 1939-1945 war memorial. A number of architects were approached to draw up various preliminary plans, but until the Gatooma Town Council had decided which particular stand to donate to the library, nothing could be finalised.

At the 1948 Annual General Meeting Mr Hodges stepped down and the Reverend C. Thorpe was elected Chairman. A Special Meeting was held in the library on Monday March 22nd to which representatives of various local bodies were invited, including the Women's Institute, Sons of England, Women's Association, British Empire Service League, the British South Africa Police Recreation Club and the MOTHS (Memorable Order of Tin Hats). All agreed to support the plan to house a memorial in the new library building in honour of the men and women of the Gatooma district who died on active service during World War II, and agreed to assist in fund raising activities towards this goal. The Police representative stated that half the proceeds of the forthcoming annual Police Ball, to be held in June, would be donated to the newly established Building Fund.

A "Gatooma Public Library War Memorial Fund" was opened and the first donation of five guineas (five pounds and five shillings) was received from the Golden Valley Sports Club, followed shortly thereafter by a cheque for £29.7s.3d from the BSAP. This was the promised half share of the profits of the Police Ball. Within a few weeks over £120 had been collected and an open appeal for donations was launched in the *Gatooma Mail*. By the end of the year the fund had reached well over £500.

The Gatooma Musical & Dramatic Society requested the loan of the library's fire extinguisher for a two night period whilst the Society staged a play at the Women's Institute Hall, this hall being situated right next door to the current library; the request was granted.

At the 1949 Annual General Meeting Revd Thorpe was re-elected Chairman, and he reported that membership now stood at 172, of which 61 were Country Members. Total library books were in the region of 12,000 and the library itself was bursting at the seams – housed in a building that could by now best be described as dilapidated. Mrs McIlleron, the current Librarian, resigned her position and was replaced by Miss Park. The magazine *Huisgenoot* was subscribed to for the benefit of Afrikaans members of the library.

In response to an appeal for funds for the proposed library, the Rhodesian State Lotteries had sent a cheque for £1,000. Architects were approached to submit suitable plans for this new building, envisaged to cost in the region of £10,000. However, the Beit Trustees, on being approached for a grant, suggested that a scaled down building costing in the vicinity of £6,000 to £7,000 should rather be considered, thus making it both easier and quicker to collect funds. And on June 21, 1949 the Chairman, Revd Thorpe, advised the Beit Trustees that the architects had been instructed to draw up plans for a building not to exceed a cost of £7,500. The Beit Trustees replied to confirm that they would donate £1,000 as soon as building operations commenced. The Gatooma Town Council donated £100 but mentioned that no further financial aid should be expected from them for at least a two year period.

In the meantime, new steel shelving arrived from England and was erected in the present library, replacing, as a matter of urgency the majority of the vintage wooden shelving which, after years of use, was in very poor condition.

Revd Thorpe was re-elected to the Chair in 1950, and announced at the Annual General Meeting that to date a little over £4,000 had been promised or actually collected on behalf of the building fund. He felt that, on the whole, public reaction to the fund had been somewhat disappointing, and more vigorous fund raising was therefore necessary.

The Gatooma Musical & Dramatic Society staged Noel Coward's popular play *Blithe Spirit* that year and donated the entire profits from the show, £68, to the Library Building Fund. And an offer of £250 for the old library building was received from the Salisbury based firm of Meikles Ltd., but this offer was not accepted.

Three tenders to construct the new library building were received from Gatooma based builders in August 1950, these were:

D. D. Jenkins £9,958, General Construction £8,738 and D. P. Scott £8,466. The committee decided to accept the lowest tender and Mr D. P. Scott, therefore, received the contract. Architect appointed was Mr Bellamy of the locally based firm of Maw, Coote and Bellamy.

Stand clearing having been completed, building work commenced shortly thereafter in order to complete as much work on the foundations as was possible prior to the onset of the rainy season (November to March). However, Rhodesia was experiencing a post-war building boom at the time and most building materials were in extremely short supply. An acute shortage of cement hampered building construction throughout the entire country.

By October the old library had found a buyer, the local building firm of General Construction having agreed to purchase the building for £2,750. Fund raising continued, donations continued to be received and on December 2nd, 1950, the lady members of the library committee organized a morning market which netted £130.

Revd Thorpe retained Chairmanship at the 1951 AGM, Mrs Dixon, a former Librarian and a stalwart member of the committee, with many years of service to the library, resigned from the committee due to her imminent departure to her new home in Umtali. She was presented with a book as a token of appreciation. Problems arose when certain members of the library raised objections to the black African assistant being in the library during library hours, and after debating the matter, the committee decided to employ an assistant Librarian to alleviate the position. With membership increasing and an expected move to the new building later in the year, Mrs Whitehead was engaged as the new Assistant Librarian at a monthly wage of £12.10s.0d. At the same time, the Librarian's monthly wages were increased to £20. Subscriptions were raised to pay for this additional expense, adults now paid £2.0s.0d. per annum and children 5/- per annum, but for those children whose parents were not library members, their junior membership fees were raised to 10/- per annum.

The Foundation Stone laying ceremony for the new library was performed by Mr Eric Fitt on Friday April 6th, 1951, at which event he paid tribute to his late mother, Mrs Amelia Fitt, whose name appeared on the stone in recognition of her twenty years of work with the library. Speaking to a gathering of some sixty people, including Mr George Munro, the local Member-of-Parliament and Mr E. P. Hay, the Mayor of Gatooma, Eric Fitt outlined the history of the library since its inception in 1917. The foundation stone itself was donated by the building contractor, Mr Dave Scott; this being his personal contribution to the library.

Work continued on the building at a steady pace, but for whatever

MR ERIC FITT LAYING THE FOUNDATION STONE WITH MR DAVE P. SCOTT ON THE RIGHT

reason which was not specified at the time, building work ground to a halt in June of that year, and it was agreed by the committee to approach the architect and request him to write a strongly worded letter to the builder, pressing him to resume work. The letter appeared to have had the desired effect and work resumed shortly thereafter, but ceased again a while later. The builder claimed that there were labour problems but that he hoped to employ additional bricklayers shortly. Due to the previously mentioned building boom, shortages of materials were compounded by a dearth of qualified and experienced labour.

In the meantime, three packing cases of steel shelving for the new library had arrived from the United Kingdom. Their cost, including customs and freight charges, amounted to £323. Mundane library work continued – it was pointed out that many members were in the habit of returning their library books well after due date, and it was agreed that a fine of one penny a day per book be levied, with a maximum of 5/- per book accruing over a longer period.

Building woes continued. It was reported that almost 1,000 roof tiles had been broken during transit between the Gatooma railway station and the building site, and replacement tiles needed to be procured, which caused a further delay. Likewise, the architect's proposed design for the Librarian's counter and grill was found unacceptable by the committee, and fresh designs were called for.

At the December 1951 committee meeting the Chairman reported that he had received a telephone call from Mr Bellamy, the architect, who told him that two members of the committee had informed him

(Mr Bellamy) of the discussion that had taken place at the previous month's (November) committee meeting concerning himself and the poor progress of the new building. The Chairman expressed surprise and concern that committee members should have shown such lack of discretion, and those present agreed that it was unfortunate that the proceeds of the committee meeting should have been divulged (leaked) in this manner.

With building work once more on track, suggestions were now forwarded as to who should perform the official opening ceremony of the new building in due course. Some members felt that His Excellency the Governor of Southern Rhodesia, Major General Sir John Noble Kennedy would be a suitable person to approach. Others felt that Lady Beit should be asked, as had already been suggested by the Secretary of the Beit Trustees. After a vote was taken, it was agreed that Lady Beit be approached to perform the honour.

At the 1952 Annual General Meeting the Reverend Thorpe once more found himself in the Chair. Mr Robert Sternberg was voted on to the committee for the first time, and he was to serve on this committee for a continuous period of no less than forty years. Whilst construction work continued at a slow pace on the new library building, which was situated close to the Civic Centre (behind the Magistrate's Court), the old library continued to function as best it could in an inadequate and outmoded building, whilst membership grew by leaps and bounds.

In June it was reported that the roof of the new library building was sagging, and a meeting with the structural engineer confirmed that it would be necessary to construct a concrete beam to remedy this problem. This was agreed upon. For reasons not stated, work by the contractor on the new building again ground to a halt, and a strongly worded letter was written to the architect to divulge the reason behind this latest stoppage. In the meantime the sum of £1,750 was received from the Rhodesian State Lotteries Trust together with a letter confirming that no further grants could be considered towards the new building.

In due course work resumed on the building, and at the December 1952 committee meeting the topic of who should be invited to perform the official opening of the new building was once more discussed. The name of Queen Elizabeth the Queen Mother was mentioned, as she was due to be visiting the country in July 1953 in order to officially open the Rhodes Centenary Exhibition in Bulawayo. This suggestion was noted, but it appears not to have been taken any further.

Revd Thorpe was re-elected in 1953, and the Librarian reported that the card index system had been completely updated and was ready for use in the new library once the move had been made. Works of fiction now numbered 7,429 and library membership stood at 251. The magazine *Stage & Cinema* was subscribed to whilst at the same time a few other magazine subscriptions were cancelled. It should be noted that, for many years, at the termination of the calendar year, magazines were sold to either library members or to members of the public, or otherwise donated to various institutions, for there were no storage facilities available to keep out of date reading material in the presently occupied and extremely cramped building.

A special committee meeting was convened on April 10th, 1953 to consider a suggestion which had come via the Civil Commissioner in Gatooma from the Prime Minister of Southern Rhodesia, the Hon. Godfrey Huggins. This suggestion expressed the view that the library committee should consider that the Misses Rhodes, nieces of Cecil John Rhodes, should officially open the new library building during the course of their visit to the colony during the month of July. After some discussion, this suggestion was turned down.

In May 1953 the Gatooma Flying Club, after disbanding its operations in the town, donated the balance of their funds, some £414, to the library, for which they were very warmly thanked. In addition, a donation of £50 was received from Mr John Mack, owner of the Golden Valley Mine (12 miles north of Gatooma) and reputed to be the richest gold mine in the country. This relatively modest contribution proved to be a forerunner of truly copious funding to be received in future years through the generosity of Mr Mack and his mine.

THE NEW LIBRARY

It was decided that the new library hours of opening for the lending section, once the move to the new premises had been made, would be as follows: 10:30 a.m. to 12.00 noon each morning – Monday to Saturday, 4.30 p.m. to 6.00 p.m. each weekday – Monday to Friday.

The Gatooma firm of J. B. Faulder & Co. was selected to supply the furniture for the new library building, and the Roll of Honour Book, bound in full Morocco leather, was ordered from the *Cape Times* printing department in Cape Town. The inscriptions in the Roll of Honour were undertaken by Mrs Margot Donnison, wife of the local dentist. It was also finally agreed upon that the opening of the new library be undertaken by the Governor of Southern Rhodesia on his next visit to the town, due in mid-September, when

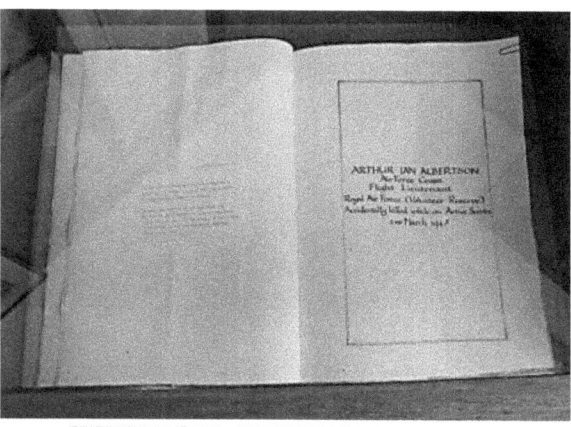

WW II ROLL OF HONOUR DETAIL

he was due to open the newly built Gatooma Municipal Offices situated in the recently and aptly named Fitt Square.

ENTRANCE FOYER OF LIBRARY

At 11 a.m. on Wednesday 16 September 1953 the Governor of Southern Rhodesia, Major General Sir John Noble Kennedy GCMG, KCVO, KBE, CB, MC officially opened the new library building and dedicated the World War Two Roll of Honour in the War Memorial section in the foyer of the library. The committee and members could feel well gratified that, after years of hard work and fund raising, the project had finally succeeded – resulting in a library that the town and district could be extremely proud of.

Members of the committee now staged their monthly board meetings in the new committee room around a large board table which must have greatly enhanced proceedings. A blip however occurred at the December committee meeting when Mr Eric Fitt wished it to be placed on record that he personally disagreed with the decision and attitude of the current Chairman (Reverend Thorpe), that he (Thorpe) had, on his own account, and without consulting the committee, banned author Nicholas Montserrat's book *The Story of Esther Costello* from the library shelves – a popular book that was in common circulation throughout the country.

Notification was received from the London office of the *East African & Rhodesian* Journal that, due to an oversight by their office, no accounts had been sent to the library since January 1948 for this publication, and would the library now please settle six years of outstanding subscriptions! The committee felt that this was an unfair demand and wrote back accordingly! Nothing further appears to have been heard from this publication's offices in the matter. It was also decided to join the newly formed Federation of Rhodesia & Nyasaland Library Association. The Reverend Thorpe informed the committee members that he had chosen a bible to be presented to the governor following the opening of the library building, apparently having failed to consult the committee on this matter.

At the January 1954 committee meeting the Revd Thorpe tendered his resignation as Chairman due to the fact that he was on transfer to Salisbury. In view of the sterling work that he had performed for the library, the committee bestowed upon him an Honorary Life Membership. At the same meeting Miss Park (Librarian) tendered her resignation and Mrs Halley was appointed in her place. Engineers from the Posts & Telephone Corporation advised the committee that, due to the fact that an entirely new cable was required to link up with the new library building, the telephone connection to the library would possibly take several months to install!

At the 1954 AGM Mr Eric Fitt was elected Chairman, a post he had last held in 1939. A new category of membership was proposed by Mr Robert Sternberg, who suggested that young adults between the ages of 17 and 21 be encouraged to join the library at an annual subscription of £1 and be able to take out two books at a time. This concession was intended to be an encouragement for them to become full members in due course. The proposal was carried and placed into effect.

In due course the telephone was installed into the office in the new building and telephone bills were duly paid for the months of September, October and November 1954 for the sums of 8/8d, 4/6d and 2/- respectively. Mrs Mawson replaced Mrs Whitehead as Assistant Librarian during the year and the black African employee was now receiving a monthly wage of £4.15s.6d plus uniform and accommodation and a bicycle allowance of 5/-. Further shelving was ordered from the suppliers in Britain. Towards the end of the year the Librarian, Mrs Halley, tendered her resignation on relocating to Bulawayo, and Mrs Mawson was appointed Chief Librarian in her place.

A subscription to the *Saturday Evening Post* increased the selection of magazines on the reading room table, and a book reservation system for members was instituted at a fee of three pence (3d) per book. Library hours were extended during the year and membership rose steadily as the town's population increased.

In January 1955 Mrs "Dickie" Matthews joined the library staff as Assistant Librarian. Mr Fitt declined re-nomination as Chairman at the 1955 AGM and suggested that this position should be rotated round the committee members. He proposed that Mr Robert Sternberg become the new Chairman and this was carried unanimously. The *Travel Book Club* was joined and *Films & Filming* and *Realities* magazines now subscribed to. *The Aeroplane*, subscribed to since 1938, was dropped. A large map of the Gatooma District was hung on one of the walls of the spacious reading room. Towards the end of the year £250 were invested with the Old Mutual Building Society at an interest rate of 3¼ per cent. The Universal Book Club was joined which enabled the library to obtain twelve books for £2.8.0d.

Mr Sternberg was re-elected Chairman in 1956. Committee members Mr Close and Mrs Olga de Meillon were requested to undertake the laying out of the library garden. Another committee member, Mr Harold Jackson, presented two Norfolk pine trees (obtained from Salisbury) which were planted in the library garden, and these trees subsequently became known as the "Jackson Pines" over the next part of the 20th century! Before long, fresh flowers from the garden were placed on the library counter on a daily basis.

The boarders of Jameson High School's girl's residence (Leander House) enrolled as junior members of the library en bloc and thereafter made good use of the facilities. In April a number of members of the Northern Rhodesia Legislative Assembly who were

LIBRARY
SHOWING ONE
NORFOLK PINE

visiting Gatooma were shown around the library and were amazed that a comparatively small town should have such an excellent library – they were most favourably impressed. Work on the garden continued and Mr J. H. "Jimmy" Beattie, one of the town's leading butchers, donated material and labour for the front and rear paved pathways. Many local residents assisted with gifts of shrubs and plants, and the lawns and flowers soon began to rival the finest gardens in the town.

Staff salaries were increased in January 1957, the Librarian now earning £22.10.0d a month. Mr Robert Sternberg was once more re-elected Chairman. At the Gatooma/Hartley Agricultural Show held annually at the Gatooma Show Grounds during the month of August, the library rented a commercial stand for the three day duration of the show in order to publicize the library and its new complex. This display, staffed by various members of the committee, proved most successful and resulted in several new members joining immediately, plus a host of enquiries and a run on application forms. A colourful exhibition of reading material, which included a goodly selection of new and forthcoming books and book covers, in addition to some of the various magazines available to members who made use of the reading room, brought in a constant stream of visitors. A little later in the year, the Governor-General of the Federation of Rhodesia & Nyasaland, Lord Llewellyn, whilst on a visit to Gatooma, had, at his own request, paid a call on the library, and was given a guided tour around the new complex. He appeared to have been greatly impressed with what he was shown.

At the 1958 AGM Mr Robert Sternberg stated in his Chairman's Report that library membership had risen by some 15 per cent, and that no less than 700 books had been added to the shelves, no mean feat, and stated that the library's financial position was sound. During the past year under review, books had been dispatched to members residing in Marandellas, Mashaba, Que Que and Salisbury, plus a number of distant mines and farms. The reading room stocked 18 various newspapers and periodicals. Mr Sternberg stepped down as Chairman and Mr A. W. Rigby was elected in his place.

In March 1958 a suggestion to purchase Afrikaans books was discussed after five Afrikaans members had brought up the subject. A resolution was passed "that in view of the fact that there was already an Afrikaans library in Gatooma (presumably belonging to the local Dutch Reformed Church), the committee does not see the need to purchase any books in the Afrikaans language." During the same month Assistant Librarian Mrs Matthews tendered her resignation, and no less than six applicants applied for her position. Mrs Talbot was chosen to fill the post. Long-time library supporter Mr Colin John Campbell donated £100 for the purchase of new books.

The committee decided unanimously that no political literature or posters should be displayed in the library. A long two tiered magazine display table for the reading room was donated by Past Chairman Robert Sternberg. Whilst Librarian Mrs Mawson went on leave, Assistant Librarian Mrs Talbot undertook her duties and Mrs Kay Strickland was appointed to take on the duties of Assistant Librarian. In September an application for the library to subscribe to the new Salisbury newspaper *The Evening Standard* was turned down for purely practical reasons. A stamp exhibition was staged at the far end of the reading room by Mr Mawson (the Librarian's husband) in aid of the proposed Gatooma Theatre building fund, the town's latest cultural project.

Mr Rigby remained in the Chair during the 1959 year. At the January committee meeting it was mentioned that "Indians, Coloureds and Africans" had been making use of the reading room and it was thought that the library policy on such use should be considered. It was decided to leave this matter for the incoming meeting to consider. However, this particular topic was not discussed again at future meetings and appeared to have fallen by the wayside.

At the February committee meeting, the Librarian posed the question as to what the position would be should she be approached by the Headmaster of Lady Tait Junior School (school for local Indian and Coloured children) with an enquiry as to whether the children would be allowed to join should they apply for membership of the library. How would such an application be treated? After a lengthy and voluble discussion, the majority of committee members voted that, under the present circumstances, the children would not be allowed to join.

The library once more staged a display of new and forthcoming books during the annual Agricultural Show and gained further members. At the end of November 1959 Chief Librarian Mrs Mawson regretfully handed in her resignation, due to the fact that her husband Arthur had decided to settle on the island of St. Helena in the South Atlantic (the island which Napoleon had been imprisoned on). It transpired a few years later that whenever the Governor of St. Helena had occasion to depart the island for periods of a short nature, Arthur was called to stand in as Acting Governor during his absence.

But despite that, we know that our former Librarian still greatly missed the Gatooma Library, which she made quite clear to friends with whom she corresponded! Current Assistant Librarian Mrs Talbot replaced Mrs Mawson as Chief Librarian and Mrs Kay Strickland was appointed Assistant Librarian.

Mr Harold S. Jackson was elected Chairman at the 1960 Annual General Meeting. New magazines subscribed to during the year included *Panorama, Personality* and *Africa Calls*. In October, the exterior of the library was painted for the sum of £65. Annual grants received by the library amounted to £125 from the Gatooma Municipality (now up from £100) and from the Government of Southern Rhodesia, the sum of £400.

Mr Jackson was re-elected Chairman in 1961, and it was decided at the Annual General Meeting that a separate "Old Age Pensioners" membership category should be instituted, with an annual subscription amounting to 10/-, plus £1 deposit fee. The weekly British *Motor* magazine was subscribed to. Once more a library display stand, manned by Librarians and committee members, was exhibited at the annual Gatooma Agricultural Show. Prominent visitors to the library during the year included the Rhodesian High Commissioner to London, Mr H. E. P. Robinson.

In January 1962 Mr Robert Sternberg drew the committee's attention to the fact that the present Library Constitution restricted membership to Europeans (whites) only, and proposed that the Constitution be amended to simply read: "That Members shall pay subscriptions to the library and conform to the rules ..." It was decided to refer this matter to the forthcoming Annual General Meeting.

Mr Jackson was re-elected Chairman at the 1962 Annual General Meeting, but no immediate action was undertaken by the committee with regard to the proposal to amend the Constitution. The *Encyclopaedia Britannica* in three quarters leather binding was purchased for the sum of £142 to replace the out of date set, and a bicycle for use by the black African assistant at a cost of £13 was sanctioned. The old set of encyclopaedias was presented to the Lady Tait School. In June the Librarian reported that magazines had been torn and stolen over the Whitsun weekend, but worse still was that the Roll of Honour had been taken out of its case and pages found crumpled, in addition to dirty marks being left on the scroll. It was agreed that a lock now be fitted to the Roll of Honour, and serious doubts were expressed as to whether the public reading room should be left open on Saturday afternoons, Sundays and Public Holidays, when the main library/lending section was closed.

When Mr Kidia, a prominent Gatooma businessman and a member of the Asian community applied to join the library in September 1962, a Special General Meeting was called which was held on Monday 1 October and attended by an all-time high of no less than 43 members. The proposed amendment to the Constitution read: Section 1, Paragraph 3. – That the word "European" be deleted. By a show of hands the amendment was passed by a majority of four votes (22 for and 18 against) and that the relevant section on membership should now read "Country Members, Ratepayers of Gatooma and such Temporary Members as the library committee may from time to time deem fit to be Members of the library". What was probably the best attended and most heated meeting ever held at the library, and which had lasted well over an hour, was finally over!

At the 45th Annual General Meeting held in February 1963 Mrs Olga de Meillon was voted into the Chair. She reported that current membership stood at 206 adults and 102 children and that a total of 375 new books had been purchased during the past year. The Chairman remarked that membership had actually decreased somewhat during the previous year and wondered whether the recently introduced television service may have been responsible for this.

At a Special General Meeting held on 22 February 1963 Mr Robert Sternberg proposed an amendment to the Constitution that: "Library Members shall consist of persons: (a) whose application for Membership has been approved by the committee. (b) Who are members on the 22 February 1963. (c) Life Members. (d) Honorary Members. That all Members shall conform to the Rules of the Library and, with the exception of Honorary Members, shall pay subscriptions to the Library". This amendment was carried by 26 votes to six.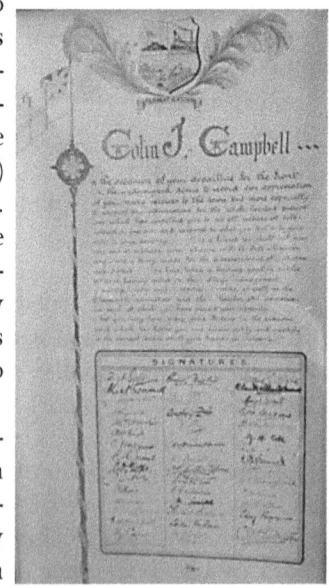

In June a donation of £1,000 was received from the Estate of the late Colin John Campbell, former committee member and staunch supporter of the library over a great many years. Subsequently a scroll given to Mr Campbell on his departure for the 1914-1918 War was offered to the library, and affixed to a wall in the library entrance hall.

The interior to the library was painted for a total sum of £178. Unfortunately, however, owing to vandalism in the reading room, these facilities would be temporarily closed out of normal library hours. In September 1963 Mr Eric Fitt resigned from the committee due to his forthcoming departure from Gatooma in order to live in Salisbury. A special vote of thanks was given to him for all the work he had performed since being elected to the committee in 1926, serving as Chairman on numerous occasions.

MRS KAY STRICKLAND

Mrs de Meillon was re-elected to the Chair at the 1964 Annual General Meeting. Past Chairman Harold Jackson passed away in May of that year. Chief Librarian Mrs Talbot resigned in June 1964 and was replaced by Mrs Kay Strickland, the Assistant Librarian. Mrs Doris Reiner in turn was engaged as the new Assistant Librarian. Monthly salaries amounted to £27.10.0d and £20 respectively. The library became a member of the Rhodesiana Society in July and in November 1964 the £125 annual grant was received from the Municipality of Gatooma.

Mrs Rose Ensor was elected Chairman at the Annual General Meeting held in February 1965. It had been the custom for many years that the serving Mayor of Gatooma be entitled to attend monthly committee meetings of the library in an "ex officio" capacity (a courtesy granted by the library) in view of the fact that the Municipality of Gatooma provided a, some may say, extremely modest grant of £125 per annum.

At the 1965 Annual General Meeting the then Mayor, Councillor Peter Horrocks, rose and stated that his Council was of the opinion that the library committee had not spent the grant received from the Council for its intended purpose, namely the purchase of books. In addition, he stated, the financial position of the library appeared to be such that a reduction or abolition of the grant might even be suggested.

Mr Robert Sternberg replied that he could not agree with the Mayor's statement. The accounts clearly showed purchases of books well in excess of the Municipal Grant. "It was difficult to pin-point expenditure against certain items of revenue, and, as the accounts closed with a loss; it was obvious that the library depended on the Municipal Grant. The library provided an excellent service for the cultural welfare of Gatooma and, therefore, Council was not burdened with any expenditure of a similar nature except for a once a year grant of £125". And he pointed out that bequests received from benefactors were intended for the benefit of the library and not of the Municipality. He advised the Mayor to inform his Council accordingly.

At the March 1965 committee meeting a black African, Mr N. J. Sibanda, applied for membership of the library, and his application was approved. At the following month's committee meeting His Worship the Mayor, Councillor Peter Horrocks (who had been absent at the March meeting) proposed that Mr Sibanda's application should be rescinded, and a secret ballot held on the matter. A discussion ensued, and an amendment was put: "That the decision made by the committee last month should stand". This amendment was put to the committee and was passed, six members voting in agreement and four against.

It was noted however at the June committee meeting that Mr Sibanda had not yet taken up his membership after a three month period, and consequently would have to re-apply under the Library By-Laws.

In August the annual Municipal Grant was received. It had been slashed from £125 to £65 pounds. A letter was sent to the Municipal Council requesting that the library grant in future be increased to, at least, the previous year's level. The library committee also put in a request to the Municipal Council to have the gravel road in front of the library tarred, as it had become a dusty thoroughfare. The Town Clerk replied that this would not be done as it was Council's intention to close off that section of road in due course.

At the 48th Annual General Meeting, held on 16 February 1966, Mrs Rose Ensor was re-elected Chairman. Mr Robert Sternberg stated that he hoped in the not too distant future a reference section would be considered, as this would be an asset to both the library and the town. His Worship, the Mayor, Councillor Horrocks then asked if it was the intention of Mr Sternberg to further bring up the question of the reference section at the present meeting. The answer was that it was only a suggestion at this stage. The Mayor then said he personally thought a reference section was an impracticable idea and that he wanted a vote on the following proposal: "That during the coming year no decision on a Reference Section should be considered". His proposal was carried by 14 votes to nine.

The following month, a letter was received from the Department of Internal Affairs regretting that the Government Grant would be cut: no amounts were however mentioned. The Municipal Grant remained at £65 for 1966, and in due course a grant of £365 was received from the government – the sum had been reduced by £85 from the previous year's figure. Committee member and former library Chairman Mr J. B. Hodges was largely responsible for obtaining an annual donation (over a five year period) of £200 per annum from the Colin John Campbell Trust, this proving a most welcome addition to the now dwindling grants. A local firm, Rhodesian Spinners, donated £150 towards the purchase of technical books, with special reference to the spinning and weaving industry. Magazines subscribed to now, included *Scope* and *Look & Listen* – the latter being the weekly Rhodesian TV and Radio Guide.

At the 49th Annual General Meeting held on the 22nd February  1967, Peter Sternberg (son of Robert Sternberg) was elected Chairman (he had been elected to the library committee at the 1964 Annual General Meeting). He proposed that as it was Gatooma's Jubilee Year (1917 1967) the library should mount a special display at that year's Gatooma Agricultural Show and highlight the fact that the Gatooma Library had also been in existence for some 50 years, having been founded in 1917. This was undertaken and many new members were signed up during the three day duration of the Show. In addition, 27 Sir John Kennedy Junior School pupils joined the library under a special membership scheme.

At the 50th Annual General Meeting held on 21 February 1968, Peter Sternberg was re-elected Chairman, and Mr Eric Barton elected Vice-Chairman. It was noted that 17 adults and 10 children had become members that month alone – a record number. *Illustrated Life Rhodesia* and *The Sportsman* joined the magazines on the reading room table and the main library lending department hours were extended for the benefit of members. The French Consulate displayed an exhibition of French books for a period of five weeks at the library during the months of April and May, and the exhibition was deemed a great success.

Unfortunately, more magazines than ever were being stolen from the reading room and the decision was taken that this room would no longer be left open except during library lending hours, when a watchful eye could be kept on readers frequenting this free facility.

The Rhodesian Board of Censors now began releasing regular lists of government banned and censored books and magazines, and the library was informed that it had a choice of dealing with any such titles in its possession by either burning them or keeping them under lock and key. The latter method was chosen. The library joined the newly instituted printing and publishing venture *Books of Rhodesia Reprint Series* in September 1968, and over the years many books from this extremely interesting series were purchased and stocked for the "Rhodesiana" section of the library. The sad news of the passing away of Mr Eric Fitt, a long serving library stalwart and Past Chairman on no less than 13 occasions, was announced at the October committee meeting. At the end of the year, adult subscriptions were raised to £5 and junior subscriptions to 10/- per annum.

The 1969 Annual General Meeting saw Peter Sternberg re-elected to the Chair, and in March he and Mr John Hodges (Past Chairman) were appointed delegates at the preliminary meeting of the John Mack Trust. Father Brosig of the Catholic Church presented a Jerusalem bible to the library as a token of gratitude for the reading pleasure that the library had afforded him during his five year sojourn in Gatooma. An en-bloc membership request from the Cam & Motor (Eiffel Flats) Library was regretfully refused as the Gatooma Library constitution did not allow this. Mrs Mary Read joined the committee in November 1969 following the resignation of Mr Jim Howard (Gatooma Town Clerk) who had left the town to settle in Bulawayo.

When handing back a book to Mrs Strickland at the counter one day, the elderly member was advised that the somewhat raunchy novel she was now returning had been placed on the Censor Board's "Banned Book List", and would therefore be placed in the "Banned Book Cupboard". "Oh no," replied the member, "I have promised my friend (another senior citizen and library member) that I would now be taking the book out in her name and take it to her, as she is simply dying to read it. I can't break my promise!!" Kay Strickland applied common sense. "By all means, let her read it, but promise me that the book will be returned to me directly when she has finished reading it." A sensible and logical decision had left everyone satisfied!

The children's section of the library had been substantially enlarged and improved, in addition to receiving a major face lift during the latter part of the year. New metal bookshelves had been installed, in addition to modern tables and chairs of different sizes to accommodate the various age groups. The children's section was officially opened on 1 December and a large selection of new annuals and books proved a major attraction to the eager young readers! At a General Meeting held on 18 February 1970, Peter Sternberg reported that the library had received a major face lift during the past year, and apart from a "new look" and enlarged children's section, an adult reference section had been started and many books had already been purchased for this most useful addition to the library. The past year had proved to be a most exciting one, especially so with the good news that the library had been left a portion of the future income of the Golden Valley Mine (through the John Mack Trust) due to the generosity of the late John Mack, part owner of the mine. Vice-Chairman Eric Barton regretfully resigned from the committee due to pressure of work.

JOHN MACK, BENEFACTOR OF THE LIBRARY

In April 1970 the first Trust received an amount of $5,200. (Rhodesia had decimalized on the 17th February 1970, two new dollars now equalled the value of the old pound). A truly golden era for the Gatooma Library had begun.

The frontage and one side of the library had been developed into lawns and flower beds and a black African gardener was now employed to tend to these. In May the first exhibition of Batik art ever to be staged in Gatooma was displayed by the artist Phyllis Taberer. Held in the reading room, the art exhibition attracted over 700 people during the five day period. A Library Commission appointed by the Rhodesian Government, headed by Sir Cornelius Greenfield, had visited the library in July and a most worthwhile meeting had been held.

In October an exhibition of local artist Rita Kajak's works and paintings, together with an opening night cheese and wine reception, was held in the library, sponsored by Gatooma Round Table. This four day exhibition likewise proved most popular and was very well attended.

NEW BOOKSHELVES

Saturday morning story telling was instituted during the year in the children's library. The library agreed to act as agent for the Bulawayo based Free Library Service, and many locals made use of this facility. In addition, the library was repainted during 1970, additional lighting was installed, a concrete apron surrounding the whole building laid, and further bookshelves were installed.

Unfortunately the annual Gatooma Municipal Grant, which had already been whittled away over the preceding few years, was now reduced to a mere $30 (£15) per annum during the 1970 year! The committee decided to return the cheque to the municipality, stating that the municipality obviously needed the funds more than the library did and, in addition, adding the suggestion that His Worship the Mayor no longer attend the library's monthly committee meetings. The Mayor resigned as a Trustee of the library and Mr J. B. Hodges was elected in his place.

Outgoing Chairman Peter Sternberg's Report for the Year 1970, read out at the 53rd Annual General Meeting held in February 1971, was a most positive one. Membership had increased and approximately 1,000 new books had been released during the year, more than in any other previous year in the entire history of the library. Of these books, no less than 300 went into the children's section. Peter Sternberg, after four years in the Chair, handed the Chairman's reigns over to Mr John Henning for the ensuing year.

After 20 years' service on the committee, Past Chairman Rose Ensor resigned in August 1971 as she was emigrating. Children's membership rose steadily throughout the year and thoughts were now given to the possibility of adding on a separate wing to the library in order to accommodate the growing junior membership. Possible further extensions to the building were likewise discussed and an architect, Mr King, was requested to draw up tentative plans. Proposed additions, apart from a children's library, now incorporated additional toilets, a dedicated committee room, a store room, staff toilets, a museum and the previously discussed reference section. Estimated cost of these extensions was calculated to be in the region of $24,000. At this stage the John Mack Trust distributed a monthly sum of $260, in addition to two half-yearly distributions; the latest October 1971 distribution having amounted to $820.

At the 1972 Annual General Meeting Mr Henning was re-elected Chairman and he reported that library membership exceeded 700. Once more, over 1,000 new books had been purchased and placed on the shelves.

At the June 1972 monthly committee meeting the question arose as to whether it would be possible for more books to be purchased from local booksellers, but as neither of the two bookshops in Gatooma, who in any case stocked only a limited number of books, had proved to be particularly co-operative, it was decided to continue purchasing books from the usual outside sources. At the same meeting the current Assistant Librarian, Mrs B. Stein, tendered her resignation. She was replaced by Mrs F. Devriendt, who was selected from eight applicants for this position.

Having now agreed to proceed with building extensions, tenders were called for and the local firm of J. B. Faulder & Co. quoted the sum of $14,885. This tender was accepted. An application for a bond was made to the Central African Building Society, but on receiving favourable overdraft/loan facilities from the Gatooma branch of Standard Bank (the library's bankers since inception), the bond application to CABS was withdrawn. Perhaps it was fortuitous that the then current manager of the Gatooma branch of Standard Bank also just happened to be a member of the library committee!

At the October 1972 committee meeting it was announced that the average monthly library income for the first eight months of the year amounted to $838 and that the average monthly expenditure amounted to $477. Building work was in progress on the new extensions. On the recommendation of the architect, acoustic ceilings were installed in the new extensions, as modern libraries deemed them superior. The committee agreed to this recommendation, and such tiles were accordingly fitted. However, Mr Hodges disagreed with the additional cost involved ($598) and felt such tiles were unnecessary. During the month of December Mr John Henning (Chief Magistrate) resigned from the Chair as he was on transfer from Gatooma.

At the 1973 Annual General Meeting Mr Robert Sternberg was voted in as Chairman and Mrs Olga de Meillon as Vice Chair. Mr John Hodges, still in part rankled by the building extensions, resigned from the committee. Building extensions were progressing well and the monthly income from the John Mack Trust had increased to $510. In addition, substantial half-yearly dividends were received.

By September 1973 the John Mack Trust distribution had doubled to no less than $1,020 per month and the half-yearly dividend received in September amounted to $5,720. Venetian blinds were installed throughout most of the library and new furniture for the children's section was received. On November 1 the new children's library was officially opened and named "The John Mack Children's Library".

New library hours were promulgated which read: Monday to Fridays: 10:00 a.m. to 12:30 p.m. and 3:00 p.m. to 5:30 p.m. Saturdays: 9:30 a.m. to 12:30 p.m. The salary of the Chief Librarian had now been raised to $150 per month and that of the Assistant Librarian to $80 per month.

A new white painted metal picket fence was erected around the entire garden, greatly enhancing its appearance. Chairman Robert Sternberg reported that the library's financial position was very sound. All building and refurbishing costs had been fully paid for – indeed, more funds were now on hand than there were prior to the commencement of building operations! Neither a Building Society bond nor a bank loan had been necessary in the circumstances. The library staff, as the Minutes reported, all received a substantial and well deserved Christmas Bonus!

At the 1974 Annual General Meeting, held on the 20th February 1974, outgoing Chairman Mr Robert Sternberg stated that during the past year membership of the children's library had increased from 152 to 220, an increase of almost 50 per cent, which boded well for the future. Mr Peter Sternberg (Robert Sternberg's son) was voted in as Chairman, a position he would hold for a consecutive 30 year period until he retired from the Chair, and for that matter, also from the committee, in early 2004.

Free library membership to selected pupils at various schools in both the town and the surrounding district were awarded in the form of reading and class progress prizes. Many underprivileged youngsters, through this scheme, were encouraged to visit a proper library for the first time in their lives, and were assisted to choose books to take out and read from a selection of books far larger than they had ever imagined existed under one roof.

In May of 1974 the Rhodesian Board of Censors mounted a travelling exhibition which they exhibited at leading libraries throughout the country, consisting of banned literature, mainly of books and magazines of a political or pornographic nature. These items were displayed one weekday afternoon on the large committee room table and the committee were invited to view them, whilst listening to an official from the Censor Board explaining the reason as to why items of this nature should, in their opinion, be banned. That afternoon there was a full turn out of committee members – it appeared that no one was going to miss out on this display at any cost! Spouses were included! And not one declined the invitation!

Whilst the government official prattled on about the dangers of Communism and pointed out the various reasons why such books and pamphlets could well turn the minds of less educated folk into becoming rabid "Reds" etc., etc., and etc. – the attention of the majority of those present – especially from some of our "prim and proper" lady members, was almost entirely focused on the lurid covers and pages of such banned reading material as *Hustler, Mayfair, Playboy, Penthouse* and similar accompanied by a selection of rather racy sounding novels! One prominent lady member was avidly seen paging through a copy of *Hustler* magazine and muttering "siss, siss" after each page, whilst at the same time making quite sure that she did not miss out on a single photograph at any stage!

A week later the library received a letter from the Board of Censors enquiring as to whether anyone had inadvertently taken a copy of *Banana* magazine from the table, as this magazine appeared to have gone missing after having been on display. I wondered whether there had perhaps been a budding horticulturist present there that afternoon??!! Tongue in cheek I posed the question at the next committee meeting, but no one owned up as having taken this magazine – that is, if there was anything to own up to in the first place!

The committee decided, in July of 1974, to sanction the construction of a mezzanine floor, which was intended to overlook the main lending section, in order to provide space for a dedicated reference section, for which there was now an urgent need. The tender for this mezzanine section was duly awarded to J. B. Faulder & Co. at a cost of $4,641.

REFERENCE LIBRARY SITUATED ON THE MEZZANINE

In August a letter was received from the Gatooma Municipality suggesting that, as the library now appeared to be in a good financial position, it should also be in a position to pay for the water consumed each month. It would appear that, since approximately 1943, free water had been supplied to the library by the Municipality of Gatooma as a token of appreciation for the cultural benefits that the library provided to the ratepayers of the town. The municipality had always contributed a fairly minimal token annual grant, which, by 1970, had shrivelled down to a demeaning $30 per annum (and had rightly been summarily rejected by the library committee at the time). Since that incident some four years earlier, the municipality had refrained from paying an annual grant, and now had the temerity to "suggest" that the library pay for the water consumed which, for a period of some 30 years, had been supplied free and gratis as a token of their appreciation! The committee wondered how low such an organization could stoop?

Needless to say, the entire library committee were against paying municipal water charges and in a letter to Council voiced their opinions in no mean terms. As no response was received, nor any water bills received, the library had obviously made its point!

An order for glass and aluminium display cases for the new exhibition room was placed with the Salisbury firm of Byfords Ltd at a cost of $2,248 and state of the art aluminium picture rails affixed around the walls of the exhibition gallery.

In October 1974 the Rhodesian National Gallery's 7th School's Art Exhibition was staged in the new art gallery and drew a first class attendance. This event was partially sponsored by the library. Library membership increased and new books were now being released at an average rate of 100 per month.

The mezzanine section housing reference books came into use during 1975. Equipped with bookshelves, two large tables and a dozen or so chairs, users could select books and read these at their leisure, for many of these expensive reference books were not permitted to leave the library. Pupils from local schools were encouraged to make use of this facility when working on specific school projects, homework and the like. These were the days prior to computers, Google, etc. and as the Gatooma Library as a whole stocked a far greater selection of reference books than most schools could afford to provide their students, our offer was happily accepted.

Two modern glass/aluminium photographic display stands were ordered and added to the exhibition room facilities. Over 200 historical photographs of Gatooma and the surrounding area were acquired during the year from such sources as the National Archives, the local Municipality and from Mr Benny Leon, a local photographer. These were to form the nucleus of the proposed archive and museum to be constructed in due course. Appeals were made to local residents to donate photographs of historical interest.

NEW SERVICE COUNTER

Almost 1,800 new books were added to the shelves during the 1975 year, and for the first time library membership reached an unprecedented 300 in the adult section and likewise 300 in the children's section.

The year 1976 saw further improvements to the interior taking place when a modern Librarian's counter replaced the current one in use. Sundry other equipment was added, in addition including the fitting of dozens of bookshelf panels to existing bookshelves in order to modernise them.

Unfortunately Mr John Hodges, the town's leading lawyer and former committee member of the library for 33 years, which included two years as Chairman (1946 & 1947), and who was still a current Library Trustee, passed away in July 1976.

1976 Exhibition of old photographs of Gatooma at the Gatooma Public Library. Benny Leon and Peter Sternberg.

An art exhibition preceded by a cheese and wine party was staged by the Lions Club of Gatooma. A medal exhibition staged by Mr Lovett (Salisbury) was held in September of that year over a five day period and attracted many viewers, over 300 alone signing the visitor's book. Mr Lovett, a noted collector, complimented the library for having by far the best display facilities in the country. This exhibition was followed in October by a comprehensive photographic display entitled "A Pictorial History of Gatooma". This exhibition was staged by Chairman, Peter Sternberg, and local photographer, Benny Leon, both of whom were interviewed on television, as a result of which the exhibition and the library received nationwide television coverage and publicity. Well over 1,000 adults, plus numerous schoolchildren attended this display during its three month run.

The October 1976 monthly committee meeting, saw preliminary

MEMBERS' READING ROOM

discussions being held with regard to possible further extensions to the library. Various ideas were introduced by Mr Robert Sternberg, which centred around a members' only reading room, an archive storage room, an Aviation Gallery and possible further extensions to the lending section.

Merit Awards in the form of free one year junior memberships were again presented to five local schools. In addition, book prizes were presented to winning participants of a local music festival, and books were also donated to the winners in the Junior Arts Section at the Gatooma/Hartley Agricultural Show.

The year 1977 saw the 9th Annual Rhodesian Schools Art Exhibition on display at the library from the 2nd to the 5th February. This proved to be a popular event, with local schools supporting this exhi-

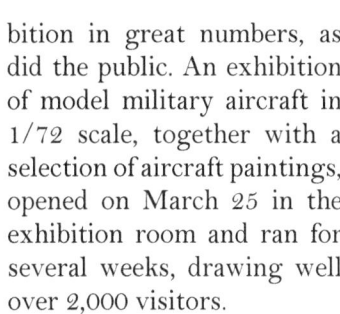

bition in great numbers, as did the public. An exhibition of model military aircraft in 1/72 scale, together with a selection of aircraft paintings, opened on March 25 in the exhibition room and ran for several weeks, drawing well over 2,000 visitors.

The Que Que (Kwekwe) based architectural firm of Victor Jenkinson & Son were contacted to draw up plans for the proposed library extensions. Suitable plans were drawn up and found acceptable. The tender for this project, which worked out to be in the region of $44,000, was awarded to Messrs. J. B. Faulder & Co. Building work commenced in August 1977.

A "Time Capsule" was prepared. The items selected in order to be unearthed "one day in the future" were sealed in a metal trunk and buried in one corner of the foundations whilst the concrete was being poured. Many items were selected to be placed in this capsule, including copies of the *Gatooma Mail* and the *Rhodesia Herald*, local school yearbooks (all newspapers, periodicals etc. were carefully sealed in plastic), petrol coupons (fuel rationing was then in operation), various photographs of Gatooma, plus a history of the town, Municipal brochures, a set of Gatooma Library Minutes, local theatre programmes, a set of current Rhodesian postage stamps plus various items of everyday use.

Mr Alan Rich, Officer Commanding Gatooma Police, and a former member of the library committee, presented a set of Purnell's *New English Encyclopaedia* to the library. The late Mr Sam Hasson, a local businessman of many years' standing, bequeathed $200 to the library in his Will, and a cheque for that amount was received from his Estate.

A sense of anticipation greeted the 1978 year. No less than 30 large bookcases for the enlarged new section were ordered from Alpha Steel in Bulawayo. A cheque for $12,650 was received in the form of a "special distribution" from the John Mack Trust.

To celebrate and introduce the opening of the new extensions, which virtually doubled the floor space of the lending section, library members were treated to cheese and a glass of wine when visiting the library over the three day period 20th, 21st and 22nd July 1978. Specially designed glass topped tables and comfortable chairs awaited users of the carpeted, well-lit and airy members' reading room. The tables displayed a wide selection of current local and overseas newspapers and periodicals, in-

cluding the *Sunday Telegraph, Time, Newsweek, Popular Mechanics, National Geographic, Punch* and a host of others.

SELECTION OF LARGE PRINT BOOKS AND CLASSICS HOUSED IN THE NEW LARGE PRINT SECTION

A separate room housed the large print books, this section proved a blessing to sight impeded and elderly members, thus aiding and retaining many members to continue reading and enjoying books. In later years a visiting Librarian from a major city in the United Kingdom congratulated our Librarian on the number and selection of large print books stocked by the Gatooma Library, stating that it was the largest display of large print material he had seen in any library situated outside of a few major cities in Britain. Praise indeed!

A new public reading room, featuring a door leading directly out to Harvey Street, was opened to passers-by, who initially made good use of these facilities. A separate committee room featured a large boardroom table plus over a dozen chairs, enhanced the quality of meetings, and the Head Librarian/Secretary's office was carpeted. The children's library was enlarged, now incorporating the space that had previously been used by the former public reading room.

It was proposed by Mr Robert Sternberg that consideration should be given with regard to expanding the library's exhibition facilities, with the suggestion that an interlinked art gallery cum auditorium, archive section and museum, which would incorporate a separate exit

MAGAZINES AND PERIODICALS IN THE PUBLIC READING ROOM

from the museum to the street, be constructed. In view of these suggestions, a Special Committee Meeting was held on 28 August 1978, and after hearing Mr Geoff Williams (representing construction company J. B. Faulder & Co.) expound on the plans for this new section of the library, it was unanimously agreed that these extensions should be constructed, their estimated cost working out in the region of $53,000. As these funds were already available, there would be no need to source additional finance.

The Gatooma Library, from its very inception, prided itself on the quantity and quality of the magazines and newspapers it provided in its reading room. However, with new monetary restrictions being imposed by the government, which affected both institutions and individuals as to how much valuable "foreign currency" they were permitted to submit overseas per annum in order to subscribe to magazines and newspapers, it appeared that the liberal display of these items would soon disappear from our reading room tables, as had already happened in other libraries throughout the country. Something obviously had to be done to rectify this!

Members of the library, non-members, friends, relatives and acquaintances were approached in order to ascertain whether they themselves personally subscribed to foreign reading material (newspapers and/or magazines). The great majority did not avail themselves of this, rather limited, facility. It was, therefore, decided to implement a scheme that would allow the library, quite legitimately, to continue to subscribe to all the foreign magazines and newspapers as had been done in the past. A tremendous amount of time, patience and energy was spent on getting this scheme underway, but it worked, and worked well. Whereas other libraries throughout the country virtually ceased to provide foreign newspapers and magazines in their reading rooms, visitors to the Gatooma Library were astounded to see that a dozen or more overseas and regional publications were available, including the very popular British newspaper, the *Sunday Telegraph*, which virtually almost every reader made a beeline for! No wonder the Gatooma Library was described as the best small town library in Southern Africa!

Before 1978 came to an end, a number of further exhibitions were staged, including a toy exhibition, which rounded off a most successful year. No less than 2,400 new books had been purchased and added to the bookshelves, and membership rose to an all-time high of 879 (407 adults and 472 children).

In January 1979, an invitation was received by the library to attend the Rhodesian History Society Annual General Meeting in Salisbury, of which organization the library was a member. The meeting was due to commence at 5 p.m. but unfortunately this offer was not taken up, as the return journey would have meant travelling after dark which, by 1979, was not recommended due to the security situation prevailing throughout the country.

It was decided to bind the collection of *National Geographic* magazines already held by the library (covering the period 1975-1978) and eventually place these bound issues (consisting of six issues per binder) in the members' reading room. As this particular monthly magazine had always proved to be extremely popular with readers, a proposal was put forward that the library attempt to procure all issues going back to January 1930 in order to build up a comprehensive collection. This little undertaking, in the end, turned out to be no small feat. Initially a number of back issues were donated by locals, and a further number were purchased from second-hand bookshops in Salisbury. This publication, after all, was reputed to be the world's most collectible magazine, and most second-hand bookshops stocked piles of these monthly magazines with the familiar yellow cover. Second-hand bookshops in South Africa were contacted by mail or visited personally, and these netted further back numbers. But now the real challenge set in. Various leading second-hand bookshops in the United States were contacted, as the older issues (the 1940's and the even rarer 1930's editions) now required to be tracked down. This hunt went on for a few of years, but in the end, with dogged determination, all issues were traced. The intricacies involved in this saga are too many to relate, but the goal was finally achieved, despite a number of hiccups along the way!

In the meantime, work had commenced on the latest extensions to the library, the exhibition wing. In January 1979 Mrs Elizabeth Rail was appointed to the position of Library Secretary and part-time Assistant Librarian to Mrs Kay Strickland, whose work had been increased having to attend to the library's ever increasing membership. Since 1975 two hardworking ladies, Mrs Etta McKenna and Mrs Esther O'Hagan had shared the posts of Assistant Librarian and Children's Librarian. The enlarged children's section was extremely well patronized, with children queuing to enter the building at opening times in ever larger numbers, especially during school holidays.

Artist Rita Schubert (Kajaks) was commissioned to paint (from archive photographs) a number of Gatooma's older and now demolished buildings from an earlier period of the town, intended for display in the library.

THE OLD LIBRARY PAINTED BY RITA KAJAKS

In August Mrs Betty Conway, a local journalist, was approached to look into the possibility of writing a history of the Gatooma Library. She promised to look into the matter but, unfortunately, nothing further materialised in this respect. Children's Librarian, Mrs O'Hagan, resigned in June 1979 and Mrs Patricia Merrick was appointed in her place.

The committee agreed to have a fountain installed in the front garden of the library, with flood lights installed to light the entrances to the building.

EXHIBITION WING

The new exhibition wing was officially opened with a cheese and wine affair held on Thursday 18 October 1979, and cheese and wine was made available to visitors to the library on both Friday 19 and Saturday 20. In its inaugural presentation, the new art gallery hosted an exhibition of photographs of early Rhodesia entitled, "The Adventurous Years". This exhibition was staged by the National Gallery from Salisbury. In conjunction with this exhibition, the library staff mounted a display of vintage china in the exhibition room, safe behind lock and key in the newly acquired glass and aluminium display cabinets. Both displays ran for a month and were very well supported. The Rhodesiana Society requested the assistance of the Gatooma Library to choose a new name for itself as it was obvious that the country's name of "Rhodesia" would be changed. The Chairman suggested "National Heritage Society". In due course the society's name was changed to, "The History Society of Zimbabwe" and its annual journal was renamed *Heritage of Zimbabwe*.

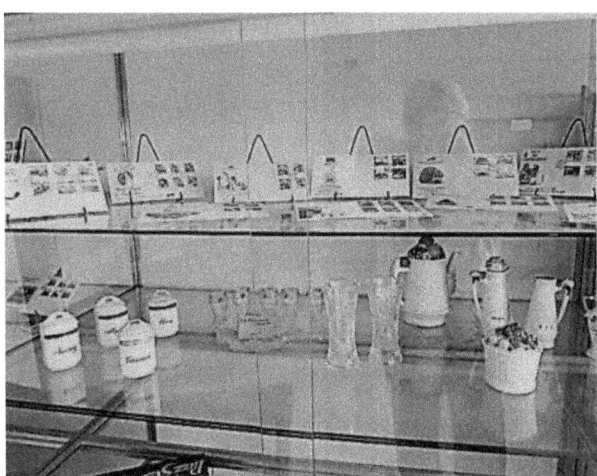

The art gallery had been fully carpeted and the latest "state of the art" picture rails installed, identical to those in a recently constructed art gallery in London. When doubling as an auditorium, the space

**ART GALLERY SHOWING PROJECTION ROOM ENTRANCE
& ENTRANCE TO AVIATION GALLERY**

available would seat an audience of 80 people in comfort, and 90 to a 100 if required. An order for modern and comfortable stackable chairs was placed, and in due course a speaker's podium was constructed to our specification. Lighting facilities were first class. At the far end of the room a door led one up a few steps into a slightly raised projection room which in due course would house two 16mm film projectors. And to crown it all, it was planned to fully air condition the entire art gallery/auditorium the following year, which would make this venue extremely popular – especially during the hot summer months!

Mrs Kay Strickland resigned from the library in November 1979 on her imminent move to Salisbury, and she was profusely thanked for her devotion to the library for a period of over 20 years, the last 16 as Chief Librarian. The library had grown out of all recognition during her time in office and her familiar and highly efficient presence would be sorely missed.

The position of Head Librarian, following Kay Strickland's departure, was offered to Mrs Etta McKenna, the Assistant Librarian, who, unfortunately, declined this promotion, due to the fact that she was not keen to take over the responsibilities that such a position demanded. As no other suitable candidates could be found, the Head Librarianship was offered to Mrs Elizabeth Rail. She accepted the position and settled down behind her desk, where she remained during the major part of the day, seldom venturing out of the office unless specifically called to do so. From time to time, when Mrs McKenna found herself under pressure at the library counter, she would vacate her desk and assist for a limited period, but soon, thereafter, would return to the sanctity of her office. This method of operation continued for some weeks and did not prove at all popular with the hard working staff. Complaints were duly lodged and discussed in committee. Despite being spoken to, she insisted on spending most of the day rooted in her office. She made it quite clear that she intended to run the library in this fashion, and would not be deterred by suggestions that she do otherwise! And when, in due course the Chairman mentioned that an exhibition was to be held in one of the exhibition rooms the following month, and that the exhibitor would be contacting her shortly in that respect, she made it abundantly clear that she considered herself solely responsible for the running of the library, and the library only. She point blank refused to have anything to do with any of the exhibition facilities at all! And the impression given was that, whether the committee accepted her decision or not, she had no intention whatsoever of changing her mind!

Urgent action needed to be taken. At the next meeting of the committee the decision was taken to send her a letter of dismissal without any further ado. The next day, letter in hand, it was placed on her typewriter, on which she was typing a letter, and she was asked to open the sealed envelope. "What is this about?" she queried, and was told that she would soon find out. To say that she was annoyed would have been a gross understatement! "You cannot do this to me," she stated defiantly, but she was assured that the committee was quite within their rights to do so. To cut a long story short, Mrs Rail departed the library shortly thereafter and the usual happy atmosphere was restored.

A week or so later the committee was tipped off "through the grapevine" that Mrs Rail intended to approach the Mayor of Gatooma to gain his endorsement and support regarding a petition that she had organized in order to compel the library to: a) withdraw her dismissal letter and b) reinstate her as the Chief Librarian! The Chairman acted on this report by phoning the current Mayor in Office, Councillor Rex Guest, in which he fully explained the circumstances and reasons leading up to her dismissal. He thanked the Chairman for putting him in the picture, and said that he would personally deal with the situation. Nothing further was ever heard in this matter.

As the year drew to a close, a number of violent incidents occurred throughout the country, one of which occurred at the Mambo Press printing works, situated on the outskirts of Gwelo. This establishment, run by the Roman Catholic Church, had been utilised by the Gatooma Library for several years to bind volumes of various magazines, amongst them being the recently acquired National Geographic Magazines, which were being bound six issues at a time, namely January/June and July/December of each year. One dark night, a number of grenades/petrol bombs were thrown into these premises, causing considerable damage to both printing machines and contents, which included a number of the library's National Geographic magazines. The hunt for replacement copies continued, and eventually all burnt and damaged magazines were replaced.

A lockable, glass fronted bookcase was ordered and housed in the members' reading room, in which the bound volumes were placed after they had been collected from the printing works. Visitors to the library marvelled at this comprehensive collection of National Geographic magazines, the largest they had ever seen!

A NEW ERA – ZIMBABWE

The library continued to prosper. In April 1980 the country changed its name from Rhodesia to Zimbabwe, under what was virtually a completely new government. A new era had begun. No one quite knew what to expect of the future, but at this time the library certainly faced an exciting future of its own. Unfortunately, in August, the news was received that Mrs Olga de Meillon, former Chairman and long standing committee member, had passed away.

It had been decided to house a large personal collection of scale model military aircraft in the new adjoining gallery which led off from the auditorium, and this new section was now aptly named the Aviation Gallery. Suitably designed glass and aluminium display cases were ordered from Byfords, a Salisbury firm, and on arrival by road transport, these attractive cases were assembled and fitted into this recently completed gallery.

Irene Sparks, a well-known local artist and the art teacher at Gatooma's Jameson High School, held a most successful art exhibi-

A SECTION OF MR PETER STERNBERG'S
DISPLAY OF MODEL AIRCRAFT

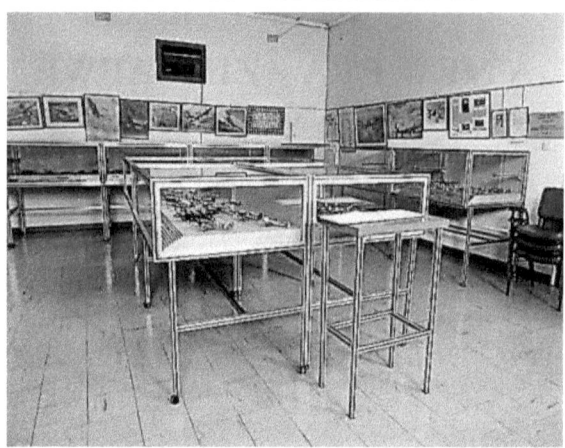

tion under the name of the Hartley Studio. Mr Christopher Till, Director of the National Gallery of Zimbabwe, officially opened the exhibition and showered high praise on the library's new art gallery and its overall display facilities.

No less than 150 dolls went on display behind secure glass display cases in the Exhibition Room a little later in the year. Although the Aviation Gallery opened its doors to the public on 18 October 1980, with an initial 350 models on display, it had been decided to perform the official opening ceremony at a later stage once a suitable person had been found to perform such duty; preferably a well-known aviator. The Chairman had someone in mind, but declined to divulge a name at this stage! Artist Irene Sparks contributed to the enthusiasm which local residents felt about the new library building extensions by volunteering to paint large murals on the exterior walls of the exhibition sector. These colourful and striking murals proved very popular indeed and remained there for many years, reminding residents of the cultural facilities that the town could rightly be proud of.

In due course the chairs that had been ordered earlier in the year arrived, and, after being placed in position, transformed the art gallery into an auditorium. When in use as an art gallery, the chairs were removed and placed in a storage section of the library. Towards the end of the year the air conditioners were delivered and installed in the various new galleries and the film projectors were received and placed in the projection room.

Despite the fact that most of the committee's attention had been taken up by the new exhibition centre and its fittings and furnishings during the year, the requirements of readers had not been forgotten! Far from it, for an almost unbelievable number of books totalling some 3,700 had been added to the shelves. At the same time, membership of the library had risen to no less than a combined 959 adults and juniors – an all-time high.

Now that the Rhodesian bush war had come to an end, matters stabilised throughout the country. No one could predict the future, but one could at least hope for the best. For those who had not emigrated, life went on, with the added benefit that the tension of the war had finally been dissipated. Having invested so much time, money and effort into building up the Gatooma Library (soon to be changed to Kadoma, courtesy of the new regime) the benefits of this decision began to show fruition.

The year 1981 commenced well. The "Paul Nash" Photographic Exhibition visited the town and held a month long showing of an interesting display of photographs in the art gallery. The library agreed to accept bookings for the town's Campbell Theatre, a recently built modern complex seating no less than three hundred theatre-goers. This theatre, initially constructed from funds raised by the residents of the town, had fortunately been included as a beneficiary of the John Mack Trust, thus joining the library in receiving copious funding. The theatre itself had been named after Colin John Campbell, the same person who had supported the library in past years. This theatre stood second to none when compared to any other theatre in the country, including theatres situated in the two major cities. A section of the Secretary's office in the library was converted into a box office which featured a glass fronted counter, manned at times by a member of the theatre but usually by one of the Librarians. In this way, many theatre-goers arriving to book seats and collect their tickets for shows were introduced to the Gatooma Library, sometimes for the first time and, having been shown around this impressive new complex, often decided to join and become members of the library.

Sound equipment was installed in the auditorium. The French Embassy and the Alliance Francaise, based in Harare, agreed to supply both classic and modern 16mm French movies, which were screened in the air conditioned auditorium on a monthly basis on Sunday afternoons to a discerning audience. In fact, 16mm film shows became a regular feature of the library, often screened on a Friday night, and no less than 26 evening film shows were shown in

MR VIV
ATWELL'S GEM
STONE
COLLECTION

1981 alone. During school holidays, suitable film shows were screened on Saturday mornings for junior members, which considerably helped swell membership in the children's section.

Well-known local prospector Viv Attwell staged a display of gem stones in the exhibition room, which attracted a steady audience and proved popular with the public.

In April 1981 the Aviation Gallery was officially opened by no less a personality than Group Captain Leonard Cheshire VC, who, when promoted to this rank, turned out to be the RAF's youngest Group Captain at the time. He also turned out to be RAF Bomber Command's highest acclaimed pilot of World War Two. Founder of the Cheshire Homes for the terminally ill, he was visiting Zimbabwe for a few days on official business with regard to these Homes, and agreed to pay a short visit to Kadoma to open the Aviation Gallery. Due to fly from Harare direct to Bulawayo on a regular commercial flight, plans were made for him to fly on a specially chartered flight from Harare to the Eiffel Flats air strip, where he was collected by Mr Robert Sternberg and driven to his home, where he and his party were provided with breakfast prior to being driven to the library.

There, Group Captain Cheshire addressed a packed auditorium of some hundred invited

PETER STERNBERG
AIRCRAFT COLLECTION
OFFICIALLY OPENED
BY
GROUP CAPTAIN
LEONARD CHESHIRE V.C., D.S.O., D.F.C.
ON
10th. APRIL 1981

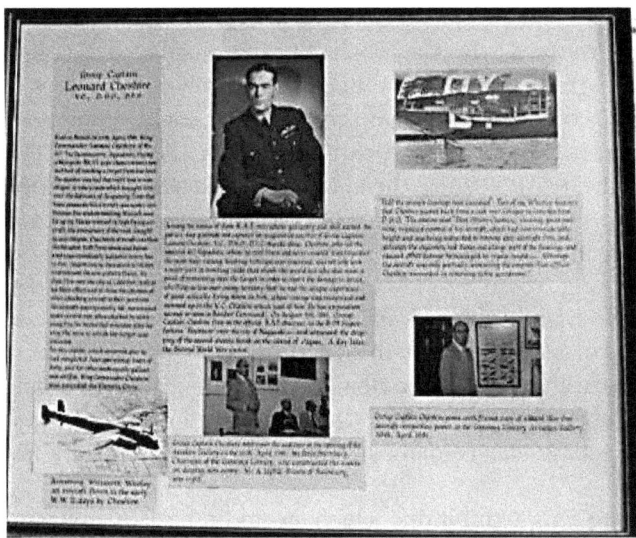

PHOTOGRAPH COMMEMORATING THE OPENING OF THE AVIATION GALLERY BY GROUP CAPTAIN LEONARD CHESHIRE VC

guests, including Zimbabwe Air Force officers from a nearby air base, together with prominent citizens, with a most enthralling talk. Thereafter, he addressed one hundred senior pupils from Jameson High School for a further half an hour in the auditorium. One could have heard a pin drop during both talks. He then proceeded to the Aviation Gallery where he officially opened the model aircraft display in the company of the town's recently appointed Mayor, Councillor Manjoro. Despite being constantly reminded by his aides that he had a plane to catch in order to arrive in Bulawayo in time for his next engagement, the distinguished visitor (he was later to be honoured with the title of Lord Cheshire) insisted that he needed time to view the entire library complex! And this is exactly what he proceeded to do! It was a very relieved accompanying party that finally managed to whisk him away! Without a doubt the event had proved to be a red letter day for the Gatooma Library.

Further exhibitions were staged for the benefit of the public. Jameson High School staged their annual art and craft exhibition at the library, attracting a larger audience to this exhibition in comparison to previous exhibitions displayed on school premises. The Italian Embassy sent down an exhibition of Italian Graphic Art, which proved popular. This was followed by a display of French Revolution period art exhibited by the Embassy of France.

Later in the year the Campbell Theatre displayed a collection of theatre programmes, memorabilia, photographs and posters of previous stage productions seen on the Gatooma stage, some going back to the 1940s. These items originated from the two locally based amateur theatrical groups, the Gatooma Musical & Dramatic Society and the "Follies". The latter group specialised in annual revues and pantomimes which they performed on the stage situated at one end of the dining room of the town's Grand Hotel. Items from the Musical & Dramatic Society covered plays and operettas produced on the stages of both the Women's Institute Hall and the Grand Hotel. Both societies moved to the newly constructed theatre when it was officially opened at the end of 1960 under the name of "Playhouse", which of course was re-named "The Campbell Theatre" a few years later.

Following this exhibition, which brought back many happy and nostalgic memories to participants in these stage shows, be they actors or actresses, directors of these productions, back stage crew and other helpers, plus the ticket paying public who had wholeheartedly supported these productions over the years, the library was approached by the Campbell Theatre management to house the entire theatrical collection in the newly established archive section of the library, and there they were safely deposited.

At the 1982 Annual General Meeting Chairman Peter Sternberg informed those present that membership of the library totalled 1,133 (adults and children combined) – the first time ever that membership

of the library had exceeded 1,000. He also drew attention to the fact that many large print books had been added to the shelves through a special arrangement made with a Harare bookseller, and it was understood that this section was the best equipped of any library in Southern Africa, judging from comments made by visitors from other centres. Among those voted onto the library committee that year was Dr Howard Cottrell (a future Chairman of the library).

Mr Viv Attwell appreciated the fact that many viewers had enjoyed seeing the gemstones he had displayed earlier, and decided to donate his collection to the library for permanent display. This offer was gratefully accepted, and a specially made glass display case with internal spot lights was ordered from Harare. The gem stones, together with a collection of interesting and colourful rocks were housed in this case, which was placed in the library reference section. In due course many visitors, some from various parts of the country, paid special visits to Kadoma in order to view this most interesting collection.

In April 1982 membership subscriptions were raised to:
Adults: Z$16.00 per annum
Students: Z$ 5.00 per annum
Children: Z$ 2.00 per annum

News was received that the John Mack Trust had decided to reduce its monthly grant to $1,020 – a cut of 50 per cent. However, a Government grant amounting to $800 was received for the 1982 year. During this period a number of library staff members resigned, due to a large extent to emigration which had become quite prevalent throughout the country. Experienced Assistant Librarian, Mrs Etta McKenna, largely held the lending section together during this period, for which the committee were most grateful, however, she regretfully again declined the position of Chief Librarian when it was offered to her. This position was eventually filled by Mrs Leonore Aitken, after a number of applicants had been interviewed for this post.

It was decided to change the name of the library from the original "Gatooma Public Library" to read "Kadoma Library", thus dropping the word "Public" and amending Gatooma to now read Kadoma, the town's name change having recently been decreed by the new government, following the country's independence from colonial rule.

With foreign governments once again establishing diplomatic relations and re-opening embassies in the country, Chairman Peter

Sternberg paid a visit to the newly established United States Information Service offices in Harare with a view to having them bring their recently advertised Space Shuttle Exhibition, then on display in Harare, to the Kadoma Library. Having successfully convinced their head of department that the Kadoma Library possessed ideal facilities to display this modernistic exhibition, the entire exhibition was in due course transported to Kadoma. Displayed at the library for a period of time, this exhibition attracted a large number of visitors and introduced and explained the space age to a myriad of local schoolchildren.

Three further exhibitions were staged during the latter part of the year, a sugar art exhibition displayed by a local prize winning sugar art specialist, a hobbies exhibition, followed by an art exhibition presented by pupils of Jameson High School.

A number of recently published books in the local Shona (African) language were purchased and it was hoped that these books would prove popular with readers of Shona. Surprisingly enough, hardly any of these books were ever glanced at, never mind taken out and read, despite the fact that they were prominently displayed on a bookshelf adjacent to the checkout counter.

Membership of the library began to decrease slightly towards the end of the year and this was attributed to the fact that quite a number of people were leaving Zimbabwe, based on a variety of reasons. It was also noted that bookshops throughout the country were importing fewer and fewer new books, thus causing a shortage of sufficient material to both satisfy readers and likewise stock library shelves throughout the entire country.

POST INDEPENDENCE

Early in 1983, news filtered out that a museum would hopefully be established within the confines of the library, which resulted in a number of historical artefacts being donated towards this venture. A major one proved to be an early printing press as used by a well-known former resident of the town, Pastor O. B. Teichert, minister of the Apostolic Faith Church in Gatooma, on which he printed his church newsletters. In due course, an appeal was launched for old photographs and other memorabilia going back to the turn of the century, and soon vintage typewriters, a selection of cameras and many other items were being donated in anticipation of this planned-for town museum. The idea of a museum had not exactly been a new one, for in past years the Municipality of Gatooma had been approached to establish a museum of the town. Unfortunately nothing ever materialised in this respect, and the library committee had finally decided to step in and provide a museum which they felt the town deserved. A sub-committee was duly set up to discuss this new venture in detail.

The purchase of a computer for library use was discussed at a committee meeting, and in due course opinions were sought into possibly indexing the books onto a computer system. Mrs Aileen Bennett was appointed Library Secretary. Magazines continued to arrive much to the delight of readers and during the year began to receive the air-mail edition of the British *Sunday Telegraph* which brought readers right up to date with the latest news.

An embroidery exhibition was the first exhibition staged in the library during 1983. This was followed in due course by a United Kingdom Poster Exhibition, brought across by the British Council (based in Harare) and this event was preceded by a cheese and wine party provided by the Council. Later in the year the British Council exhibited the Commonwealth Book Exhibition at the library, and presented the Kadoma Library with a comprehensive selection of English classics. It was noted that, due to the library's excellent display facilities, Kadoma was now receiving exhibitions that previously had only been seen by Harare and Bulawayo audiences, as other towns in the country found it awkward at times to stage some of these exhibitions. The final exhibition staged in 1983 was the Railways Memorabilia Exhibition.

The Library Box Office continued to handle Campbell Theatre bookings, and the library was also requested to handle bookings for dances and other events staged by various local organizations.

Library membership began to rise once again, and other good news was that no less than 2,797 books were received during the year. Not all were new books however, as donations of second-hand books were received from as far afield as the United Kingdom and the United States of America. Many of these were children's books, which helped boost junior membership. Likewise, many library members who were now departing the country very kindly donated their collections of books. Many of these books turned out to be either duplicates or were not suitable, and much of this material was donated to the library being established in Rimuka Township, a black African township, situated near Kadoma and administered by the Kadoma Municipal Council.

A new development occurred in 1984 when the library auditorium began to be hired out for local business seminars, training courses, conferences, Women's Institute meetings and Rotary Club functions, plus various other events. The auditorium met all the criteria for staging functions of this nature, providing excellent acoustics, comfortable seating for up to 100 people, sufficient parking facilities and, of great importance, an excellent air conditioning system highly praised and appreciated during the hot summer months! In addition, tea facilities for those attending were provided by the library staff when required.

Jameson High School staged its annual art exhibition and as usual, attracted a goodly number of pupils, parents and members of the public to this popular annual event. During the month of October, Mrs Elizabeth Prinsloo joined the library staff in the position of Assistant Librarian.

Although the library continued to receive its full complement of international magazines (plus the highly popular *Sunday Telegraph*), together with its much awaited annual quota of recently released hard back bestsellers from South Africa, the country's financial woes had seriously begun to affect the country's bookshops. The library received a letter from one of their main suppliers of books, namely Vigne Bookshop in Bulawayo, informing them that there was no longer any foreign currency available to booksellers in order to import books other than school textbooks! When a foreign currency allocation was applied for by the Kadoma Library in order to purchase books from overseas, considering that Zimbabwe booksellers no longer appeared to stock suitable books for libraries, the application was turned down. It also became apparent that, in order to save foreign reserves, paperbacks only were being imported into the country by bookshops. Despite these woes imposed on the reading public, the library nevertheless received no less than 1,213 books during the calendar year 1984 and, as in the previous year, a goodly proportion of donated books were once again re-donated to the Rimuka Library.

In March 1985 the sad news was received that Mrs Kay Strickland (Chief Librarian 1964-1979) had passed away in Harare. She had originally joined the library staff as Assistant Librarian in 1958 and had served the library for almost 22 years, providing dedicated and exemplary service throughout her time with the library.

Following a request from the library staff to the Campbell Theatre to assist them with additional manpower from time to time in manning the box office, especially during busy periods such as when heavy bookings were received prior to the National Theatre Festival being staged in Kadoma, the Campbell Theatre decided to terminate its theatre booking facilities at the library altogether. Thus an amicable arrangement, which had lasted four years and had incurred no expense to the Theatre, came to an end.

During April the British Council exhibited a poster exhibition which ran for a period of time, and a contingent of Zimbabwe Gem & Mineral Society members from Harare and other centres paid a visit to the library's gemstone exhibition. In May the library's lockable glass display cases proved their worth when a coin collection was placed on display!

The library staged an exhibition entitled "History of Theatre in Kadoma" in the exhibition room, displaying modern and vintage photographs of local stage productions, together with a display of theatre programmes, all of which brought back many enjoyable memories and much nostalgia!

A suggestion was forwarded to the committee that the library purchase school textbooks and stock them in the library for use by local school children. This suggestion was turned down as there was no intention of turning the library into a study centre.

Vandalism continued to rear its ugly head when it was found that expensive reference books had well over 20 photographs cut out of them and one book which had been partially mutilated was found with a razor blade still inserted amongst its pages.

As had been anticipated, endemic foreign currency shortages had greatly depleted the purchase of new books during the year, and shelves in bookshops throughout the country were looking decidedly bare.

The following year, 1986 saw no relief in foreign exchange restrictions, and new books were extremely difficult to source in Zimbabwe. Likewise, foreign magazines virtually disappeared from newsstands, and it looked as if the Kadoma Library members' reading room, a very popular place for members, would suffer accordingly. However, it was decided that, somehow or other, the extremely well-earned reputation established by the Kadoma Library in providing top class reading material should continue despite all the obstacles placed in its way. With a lot of organization and co-operation, details of which are not going to be divulged after all these years (and were kept under wraps at that time as well), magazine and newspaper subscriptions continued to be renewed, and the multitude of both foreign and South African magazines, including the airmail edition of the highly popular weekend edition of the *Sunday Telegraph* newspaper, continued to arrive, much to the delight and relief of library members. This resulted in a goodly number of new members joining the library for the very first time. Their sole purpose, it turned out, was to frequent the reading room on a regular basis, and they seldom ever bothered to take out library books!

But this scheme to keep the library going under all circumstances did not apply to reading room material only – for the latest in fiction, non-fiction and children's books were likewise sourced. The latest books by best-selling authors continued to appear regularly on the shelves, and visitors to the library from other towns and cities continued to marvel at the excellent selection of new books that appeared on a regular basis on the Kadoma Library "latest release" shelves. The library's reputation continued to increase!

The Women's Institute Hall having recently been sold, its foundation stone was removed from the building and donated to the library, another item received in anticipation of the yet to be established museum.

The British Council brought down their "Figuration & Fantasy" exhibition which was preceded by a cheese and wine party opening event. A few months later well-known Zimbabwe artists, Rose

O'Conner and Felicity Kirkman, staged an exhibition of their paintings, many of which were sold to appreciative purchasers.

Due to the fact that 16mm films were now fast going out of date and movies were becoming difficult to hire, it was decided to discontinue this form of entertainment, and it was agreed that the 16mm projectors in use were to be disposed of.

However, despite the critical foreign currency shortfall, the library managed to source no less than 1,005 books throughout the year, of which some 200 were donated. And what is more, the membership of the library continued to increase, and by the end of December 1986 stood at no less than 1,326. This was the highest membership ever recorded to date.

In 1987, suggestions were put forward at a committee meeting that a video section be introduced in the library, now that the once popular 16mm film shows had been discontinued. Library Vice Chairman Dr Howard Cottrell stated that such a section would be a non-starter as the costs would be great and the library staff would find themselves overloaded with additional work. Following this advice, the majority of members present decided to drop this suggestion.

Exhibitions held in the exhibition room during 1987 included a needlework display mounted by members of the local branch of the Women's Institute, and was followed in due course by a Zimbabwe schools' badge and tie exhibition, both of which proved most interesting. The art gallery hosted two popular art exhibitions, both by local Kadoma artists. The first was staged by David Newman, who had previously exhibited his artwork at the National Art Gallery in London, and whose parents were local farmers. The second exhibition was staged by Irene Sparks, the art teacher at Jameson High School in Kadoma. Both exhibitions were extremely well supported and the majority of the paintings found buyers. Local art had certainly come into its own, and the library was congratulated on being in a position to provide first class display facilities for this standard of artwork.

In 1988 a suggestion was forwarded that a sheet music section be started at the library, and an appeal was launched for surplus score sheets. Although piano lessons were still offered in Kadoma, sheet music as such was no longer obtainable throughout the country. Unfortunately this appeal was poorly supported and in the circumstances did not succeed.

A total of six exhibitions were held during the year, commencing with staff from the Rumanian Embassy in Harare motoring to Kadoma to present a talk and poster exhibition acclaiming the joys and advantages of taking a vacation in Romania. Large and attractive posters had been mounted on the walls of the exhibition room, and the event was to be officially opened by Zimbabwe Cabinet Minister Comrade Enos Chikowore at 8 p.m. A good crowd turned up to witness this event, the first, to my knowledge, held by officials of a Communist nation in our town. Unfortunately, the Zimbabwe Cabinet Minister failed to make his way to the library (on arrival in Kadoma – well on schedule to present his address – he had been observed disembarking at a well-known hostelry) and appears to have decided to first quench his thirst at this popular motel, rather than proceeding straight to the library, where everyone was waiting for him to arrive and open the evening's proceedings. Being aware of the position, the Chairman advised the leader of the Romanian delegation to get his show on the road, which, after a time, he proceeded to do with some trepidation, ever hopeful that the Cabinet Minister would arrive at any moment. The audience was regaled about the good life in Romania, the outstanding attributes of their leader, Comrade Nicolae Ceauşescu and all the virtues of his wise leadership, that the country was a stable, peaceful and progressive one, and that tourists would be welcomed with open arms and assured of a most interesting and enjoyable vacation.

The evening's presentation had almost been concluded when Cabinet Minister Enos Chikowore finally made his appearance at the library, and he appeared to be in a somewhat jovial mood. He had, he stated, been "held up" en route to the library (which to a degree was true, in a certain sense) but declined to elaborate on the cause of this delay! In his address, which now became the closing address instead of the opening one, Comrade Minister Chikowore thanked the Romanian Government for all the assistance that they had provided to poor, struggling, little Zimbabwe over the past number of years, and that the citizens of Zimbabwe should always be grateful to such well-established and richer nations who were now helping Zimbabwe to find its own feet.

The evening now officially over, the library Chairman accompanied the Minister to his chauffeur-driven, very latest model Mercedes Benz where he settled himself comfortably onto the sumptuous rear seat of this luxurious automobile, which purred off into the night. Sometime later, having assisted the Romanians with the dismantling of their display material, the Chairman walked them to their car, an old, grey, Renault 12 sedan. Having bid farewell, all four Romanians squeezed themselves into their Renault amongst boxes of pamphlets and posters and chugged off on their journey back to Harare.

A postscript to this tale: The following year, on December 22nd, 1989, following an uprising, Romanian leader Comrade Nicolae Ceauşescu was arrested. Three days later, on December 25th and following the briefest of trials, he and his wife Elena were shot. Their progressive reign was over.

The United States Information Service staged a Photographic Exhibition, which was well received. A Mr Anderson, a visitor to this country, staged a photographic exhibition some months later, and the Women's Institute (National Headquarters) displayed their Annual Poster Exhibition over a period of time.

Some years earlier, the town of Kadoma had been "twinned" with the town of Stevenage in the United Kingdom, and it was suggested that the Kadoma Library should likewise be "twinned" with the Stevenage Library, hopefully to the benefit of both organizations. The Kadoma Library was happy to do this, and when the Mayor of Stevenage paid a visit to Kadoma during 1989, he was hosted to tea at the Kadoma Library, and was highly impressed by the library, even more so when hearing that the Gatooma Library was self-funded and did not at all rely on the Municipality of Kadoma!

A few months later some 700 second-hand books were received in a bulk container from Stevenage as a gesture of support for the Kadoma Library. Unfortunately, it turned out that the great majority of these were technical books, many of which were out of date, and so were found to be unsuitable for the library. Likewise, most of the fiction material received turned out to be duplicates of books already in the possession of the library and so, apart from a few odd exceptions, it was decided to hand over the great majority of this consignment of books to the Rimuka Library. This library, situated in the adjoining township of Rimuka, was owned and run by the Municipality of Kadoma. The books were gratefully received, and boosted the Rimuka Library's stock of books considerably. And in view of the Stevenage Library's generosity, a dozen or so newly published pictorial books on Zimbabwe relating to the country's nature reserves, wild life and tourism were in turn newly purchased by the Kadoma Library and sent to Stevenage, in the hope of boosting tourism in Zimbabwe.

Shortly thereafter, the Kadoma Library received a notification from the Kadoma Municipality that any books that were received in any future consignments from Stevenage should be handed directly over to the Kadoma Municipality, who felt that they (the Municipality) should be the sole recipients and beneficiaries of any donations from their "twin-town" in the United Kingdom! We did not bother to query the reason behind this request, and in any case, the Kadoma Library received no further book "donations" from Stevenage.

During 1989 Mrs Pamela Stead was appointed as Secretary/Treasurer of the library, following the retirement of Mrs Aileen Eakins from that position after many years of compilation of the history of the Kadoma Library. As from October 1st, 1989, adult membership subscriptions were raised to read $24 per annum, country members $30 per annum and junior members $10 per annum. Mrs Mary Palframan, assisted by a number of her junior art pupils, painted a most attractive set of murals on the exterior wall of the children's library – the section that faced Harvey Street.

MURAL PAINTED OUTSIDE OF THE CHILDREN'S LIBRARY BY MRS MARY PALFRAMAN AND HER PUPILS

Exhibitions staged during the 1989 year included a "First Day Stamp Cover" exhibition and two art exhibitions, the Kadoma/Chegutu (formerly Gatooma/Hartley) Amateur Artists Circle exhibition, and a display of Graphic Art by Miss Tamara Sternberg (the Chairman's daughter), who at the time was based in Johannesburg.

In 1990 Mrs Beulah Ashby joined the library staff as a part-time Librarian and was initially employed during weekday afternoons. In October, Head Librarian Mrs Leonore Aitken resigned and in due course moved to Scotland in order to retire. Librarian, Mrs Liz

Prinsloo was appointed Head Librarian in her place. Mr Russell Barnes, a long time committee member and current Vice-chairman and Library Trustee, resigned from the committee due to ill-health.

Exhibitions held at the library during the 1990 year saw the Indian High Commission stage a photographic exhibition titled "Nehru – His Life and Times". Following the opening ceremony, the local Indian community provided delicious snacks to the appreciative audience. The Librarian was disappointed at the lack of interest in the exhibition from some of the schools. An interesting exhibition of mementos was held in the exhibition room, and a number of minor art exhibitions were held during the remaining part of the year.

(Sheliegh Barton continues the history)

At the 73rd Annual General meeting in 1991, Mr Robert Sternberg, a committee member and often Chairman was, after 43 years of faithful service, made an Honorary Life Member of the library. Accepting the honour, Mr Sternberg reminisced about his 43 years association with the library with his usual humour. He congratulated his son, Peter Sternberg, who had to date given 18 years of service to the library. The committee wished him well in his retirement due to ill-health.

At the same meeting, Mr Russell Barnes was given honorary membership of the library as he had been a member since 1963.

The high garden expenses were discussed, but it was due mainly to the purchase of a new hosepipe and lawnmower. The problem of supplies of books was an ongoing nightmare. The prohibitive cost of new books was offset by the purchase of 400 good second-hand books. Due to the scarcity of books, a "Black List" was introduced to name and shame subscribers who either defaced books or failed to return them and the library was using the services of the Messenger of the Court more and more frequently.

Stevenage links were strengthened by a visit from Mrs Marianne Cusworth of the Stevenage Library who, at her suggestion, decided to send out a Junior Librarian, Miss Jane Tyrell, for a period of six months to assist in the Kadoma Library and that of the Rimuka and schools' libraries.

The income from the John Mack Trust was $58,757.00 – an increase of $31,517.00 on the previous year. This money was to be spent on capital expenditure and not the day to day running of the library. This was an enormous gift to the library and Mr Brocklehurst obtained relevant information on the Keetay Trust as a means of investing the monies received.

The exhibition room was used extensively during the year. There were exhibitions of beautiful embroidery from Mrs Lubbe, Mrs Hoffman and Mrs Minnaar. A history of the library was organised by Mrs Mary Read who was proving to be the backbone of any displays and a display of members' "Favourite Paintings".

A former library committee member, Mr Noel Brettell passed away during 1991. He was a well-known poet, author and staunch supporter of the library.

As 1992 dawned, even though there was still a critical shortage of books, Kadoma Library was so much better off than other libraries in the country. Despite the situation, 675 new books were purchased. The tragedy of the state of the Zimbabwean economy filtered down, seen in the enormous price of books. A new paperback book was costing in the region of $70.00. In order to keep the shelves stocked, 453 second-hand books, in good condition, were purchased. A massive blitz was undertaken to discard old books, many of which had been on the shelves since the 1940s! These were, as usual, donated to other struggling libraries. Stevenage Library sent out a huge parcel of books many of which were more like text books, so these were donated to local schools.

A visitor from the British High Commission to the library was duly impressed. He brought with him a gift of 13 very useful reference books. It is interesting to note that a stock count of books was done and the results were as follows:

	FICTION	NON FICTION
Adult	20 000	12 200
Children	8 500	2 300

This is amazing when one thinks that the books in the original library fitted into one bookcase.

The John Mack Trust injected a further amount of $105,700.00 into the coffers but, yet again, there was no grant forthcoming from government and was never to be again.

A very popular exhibition of books, poems and photographs of the late Noel Brettell was held in the small exhibition room from April through to December. This was a fitting tribute to his life organised by his son and daughter-in-law, John and Mary Brettell.

Local artists made use of the art gallery twice during the year and many were fortunate to sell some of their work. These exhibits proved to be popular with the local community who continued to support local artistes.

At the Chairman's instigation, a TV and VCR for the conference room were purchased, thus doing away with the old 16mm film projectors which were sold for $7,000.00. It was intended to hold weekly films for the junior members on Saturdays and for the public, should a popular film come to hand. Dr Cottrell was to organise the whole system even though he had been against it previously. The library was, yet again, demonstrating its commitment to progress. Also, it was the first time that the documents for the meetings were photocopied and not printed on the old duplicating machine.

Sadly, in 1992 Mr Robert Sternberg and Mr Russell Barnes both died and in 1993, the Chairman paid tribute to both Mr R. Sternberg and Mr R. Barnes – men who had been stalwarts of the library for many years. A minute's silence was held in appreciation of their many years of service to the library and Kadoma in general. Members felt that this was the passing of an era. The Chairman, Mr Peter Sternberg, announced that this was a very special AGM as it marked the 75th anniversary of the library. Seventeen members were in attendance. Mr S. Payne replaced Mr R. Sternberg on the committee. Mr P. Sternberg was made a Trustee of the library in place of his father, Mr R. Sternberg. Mrs Read commented on the favourable report of the library, made by Miss Jane Tyrell, to the Stevenage Library.

Books were more readily available in 1993 but, unfortunately, at a greater cost. The Vice-chairman, Dr Cottrell, reported that the innovation of the Saturday morning film shows, 53 in all so far, for the junior members, was a great success with an average of 30 children attending and a maximum of 60. Many of the children who attended the shows had had no previous exposure to the library and the relaxed atmosphere of the film mornings had resulted in new members signing up. The children began arriving at least an hour ahead of the opening time and the films were well received. Behaviour was generally good and it was deemed to be a great success.

The Chairman reported that in 1993 the library purchased and placed in circulation 1,022 new books but on the downside, membership dropped by 70. This was disturbing as this brought the total loss of members to 100 in two years. A concerted effort by the staff, consisting of Mrs Prinsloo, Mrs Ashby and Miss Sharon Davis, was made to encourage new members. It was thought that the current downturn in the economy was the reason for this state of affairs. The library was fortunate in that the income from the John Mack Trust amounted to $92,320.00 which, though less than the previous year, was proving a life saver.

Exhibitions were an ongoing feature of the library and Mrs Mary Read had appealed through the local press for "Favourite Paintings" and "Old Fashioned Tins" for an exhibition. This was proving very popular. Peter Sternberg staged an "Aviation Day" on behalf of Rotary, which was well attended by over 100 people. No other exhibitions were held that year. A burglary that took place at the end of 1992, where downpipes and various outside fittings were stolen had resulted in security being updated by installing security screens, bars and security doors. It was indeed fortunate that the security at the library was first class, allaying the fears of exhibitors.

THE CALM BEFORE THE STORM

Over the years, the affairs of the library seemed always to be either in a state of high or low and 1993 had been no different. At the beginning of 1994, however, exchange control on the purchase of books was, thankfully, lifted. Quick to take advantage of an opportune situation, Mr Peter Sternberg had established a contact with a leading book store in the United States and was able to maintain a steady stream of the latest fiction. Sometimes these books were on the library shelves before they were even published in the United Kingdom and, certainly, not at local booksellers and not very long after they were published. We were, momentarily, the envy of national and local libraries! Mr Sternberg was quick to point out that, from comparing the present to previous years' situations, this was a golden period for members and had to be exploited to the full. This was done by sourcing books in South Africa and accepting the steady stream of donated books. The Rotary Club of Sunnyvale, California continued to send much needed children's books. To compound this happy position, the John Mack Trust donated $190,640.00: an increase of $96,320.00 over the previous year. Happily, the Golden Valley Mine was producing well and the gold price was stable.

Following on from attempts to increase membership as mooted at the last year's AGM, the staff had worked out various new options for membership. Single membership and composite memberships were introduced with an increase in the number of books allowed out at any one time. This proved popular with the public and compensated for the slight increase in membership fees. An aggressive programme was launched to encourage new members and for the first time in many years, the membership exceeded 1,000. The staff at that time were assisted by Brenda Stead, Pam Stead and Aileen Eakins, who were all part of a most efficient team. In an effort to encourage literacy in children, a short story competition was held with very disappointing results. Only seven entries were received.

A three week visit from Mrs Ann James, the Chief Librarian of the Stevenage Library was very beneficial to the staff. Her new ideas were welcomed by a staff eager to embrace any innovations that might increase the efficiency of the library. She was hosted by the Chairman and his wife who later visited Stevenage and linked up with previous staff exchanges, who had assisted Kadoma Library over the years.

Vandalism reared its ugly head in the public reading room as it did all those years ago. The scope of the theft was amazing, as by the end of the day, most of the periodicals and newspapers set out that day, were stolen. Whole sections were being cut out of the newspapers. A record was set when *Time* magazine was stolen within 20 minutes of being displayed and *The Economist* costing $23 a copy was also targeted. A disturbing aspect of this destruction was that light fittings and sockets were also stolen and it appeared that the room was being used as sleeping quarters during its opening period as greasy containers and packets littered the floor. Having a full- or even part-time security guard was too expensive. Consequently, the reading room was closed for several weeks and on being reopened was carefully monitored by the existing staff. It was history repeating itself.

1994 marked the 75th AGM of the library so another exhibition of memorabilia and old books was planned by Mrs Read to commemorate this special anniversary. This ran successfully for several months. In fact, four exhibitions in all were held throughout the year viz. "Favourite Painting", "Old and New Tins", "Old and Interesting Bottles" and "Poems on the Underground". The library was fast becoming a very important cultural venue for locals and visitors alike. At the AGM it was refreshing to note that Mr Tawona Moyo, an enthusiastic young local was elected to the committee adding a new dimension.

Membership continued to rise in 1995, mainly due to the excellent supply of books. The staff were able to continue sourcing books from the USA, Britain and South Africa and membership increased by 108 members. However, composite membership was proving popular and was also a possible motive.

The library exhibitions were becoming more and more popular in the district and a lace exhibition – staged by Mrs Stevenson – proved popular as was a toy exhibition – organised by Mrs Sheliegh Barton. But the highlight of the year's exhibitions was an excellent display of World War II memorabilia displayed by Mr Geoff Burrows and his sub-committee to commemorate the 50th anniversary of the end of the war. Photographs, medals, swords and machine guns and censored letters were on loan to the library from the public. This exhibition was on display from May until September and was well attended. In addition to the exhibits, talks and fortnightly film shows on World War II topics were screened. Mrs Hermoine Sternberg orchestrated the whole programme with the help of Mrs Prinsloo and Mrs Ashby. Most schools supported the events but, for reasons unknown, some schools boycotted the film shows.

There was no cinema in Kadoma at that time, so it was decided to hold fortnightly classic films from the 1930s to the 1950s and these were screened with good audience response. Dr Cottrell's Saturday film shows for the children continued successfully. The interest in these film shows prompted the committee to decide to introduce a video section at the library, thus keeping up to date with some libraries in South Africa and overseas. This was possibly the first library in the country to supply this facility. There was no intention to go into competition with commercial video clubs as this facility would only be available to library members and the content of the videos on offer would be classical and superior movies. It was suggested that the current "O" and "A" level English set works could be purchased. Mrs Sheliegh Barton and Dr Cottrell offered to source these videos. Mrs Sheliegh Barton volunteered to set up the administrative system and Dr Cottrell the hardware.

The committee was now in the enviable position of releasing 100 new books on the shelves each month during 1996 as well as subscribing to a good selection of newspapers and periodicals, once more. At members' requests, a tennis magazine and the local farmers magazine were added to the purchases. It was fortunate that over 1,036 books were added to the shelves. The staff continued to discard out of date and damaged books during the year. It was still possible for the library to employ a Librarian and Assistant Librarian with three cleaners, ensuring the continued pristine condition of books and surrounds. The members' reading room was still very popular and periodicals were supplied on a first come first term basis. The old discarded books were donated to various associations and a new society that benefitted from this was ZACRO – the Zimbabwe Association for Crime Prevention and Rehabilitation of Offenders. This Association was particularly interested in any non-fiction books that were discarded. In order to keep up standards, Dr Brettell had been employed to re-catalogue the non-fiction section in consultation with the Librarian.

An exciting project was suggested by the Chairman, Mr Peter

Sternberg. He would approach Mr Sam Levy, who had purchased the land and buildings in the centre of Rhodes Street that he intended to demolish, and request that he donate or the library purchase the façade of the first two storeyed building in Gatooma. This would then be built into the museum area like the original. Unfortunately, Mr Levy was, apparently, not sympathetic to the cause and sold off the granite blocks to a dealer in Gweru. However, he did give the windows and two remaining original granite blocks. Mr Bob Rogers volunteered to supervise the work of building the Fitt Building into the museum. Mr Rogers, working with old photographs managed to create an identical replica of the old building including copies of the advertisements displayed on the veranda. This work progressed well and the official opening would probably be at the end of that year. Whilst this work was continuing, essential maintenance was done on the building; the original part of which was now 47 years old and the old copper water pipes had disintegrated. Mr Ashby was responsible for the on-going maintenance work and the committee was grateful for his unceasing work in this respect.

After the very successful exhibits of the previous year, there was suddenly a lull in activity in the exhibition room but a display of a series of vintage comics owned by the Chairman, was mounted. This was particularly enjoyed by the younger members as well as the older members who were filled with nostalgia.

The video section was in place, at last, all 200 videos having been catalogued, reviewed and copied. The original concept of classics and

INITIAL DISPLAY OF THE VIDEO SECTION

educational videos had been adhered to and the shelves displayed, amongst others, Shakespeare and National Geographic videos. This took the team of Mrs Sheliegh Barton, Dr Cottrell and Mrs Pam Stead many hours. All the effort was justified as the section proved extremely popular and was only one of two library video sections in the country.

Kadoma's twin town, Stevenage, issued an invitation to Mrs Elizabeth Prinsloo, the Librarian to visit their library. Her air ticket was purchased by the Kadoma Library but her accommodation was arranged by Stevenage. This was a very interesting trip and Mrs Prinsloo returned from her visit with many new ideas. Whilst she was away, volunteer members assisted at the counter.

Mrs Aileen Eakins audited the library books each year on a voluntary basis continuing the tradition of community spirit.

Some months after Mrs Prinsloo's return, the Mayor and a party of councillors from Stevenage, visited the library facility and were duly impressed. Trish Mbanga, the organiser of the Annual Book Fair, also visited the library and as a result the library had a request for a possible visit from the Librarians' Association of Zimbabwe.

THE STORM

As the months went by in 1997, the financial position of the library was under stress, yet again. The funds from the John Mack Trust were severely curtailed by the drop in the gold price and the fall in the value of the dollar sent the cost of books spiraling once again. The committee reluctantly decided to increase the subscription fees. The facts at that time were that in 1997 a year's subscription was $200 per annum and yet a new hardback novel was selling for $500 per copy and the cost of books was predicted to rise by 40 per cent. The great majority of members appreciated this increase as an attempt to keep the library a viable concern. The costs of the ever popular mailing of library books to 14 postal members had risen from 65c per book to $3.00 per book. As several hundred books were mailed per year the new postal charges proved to be an expensive burden.

The National Gallery of Zimbabwe was keen to purchase land in various centres in order to erect art galleries. To this end, the municipality suggested that we donate an area of library land adjacent to the existing buildings for this purpose. After much discussion it was decided not to commit the library to this scheme until more facts were available. Following on from the financial constraints in the previous year, 1998 was a year of consolidation. Libraries throughout Zimbabwe were under pressure, many stating that due to financial constraints they could be forced to close down, hence the policy of restraint in Kadoma. Only 365 new books made it onto the shelves but 480 really good second-hand books were donated. The staff comprising Mrs Prinsloo, Mrs Ashby and Messrs Alois, Ephraim, Godfrey and Mrs Pam Stead kept up the library standards with almost fanatical zeal.

Despite the financial gloom, there was ongoing activity at the library. The auditorium was hired out on a regular basis to commercial undertakings, private organizations and service clubs. The strenuous efforts of the Chairman resulted in the municipality re-surfacing the parking area. Mrs Sheliegh Barton produced a brochure on the library facilities which was well received.

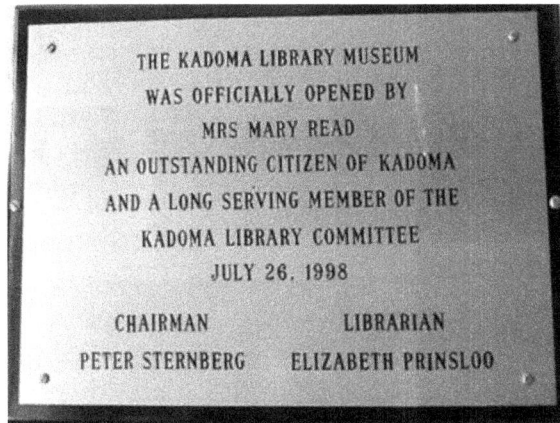

The highlight of the year had been the official opening of the Fitt Building in the museum on the 26th of July by Mrs Mary Read, whose mother, Mrs Davies, had been a Librarian in the old library in the 1940s. It was a gala affair with 100 invited guests from all parts of the country. Mrs Mary Read unveiled the plaque to commemorate the opening of the museum and Mr Bob Rogers, who was mainly responsible for the erection of the building, unveiled the plaque commemorating the opening of the Fitt Building façade. The exhibits in the museum were varied and the visitors were very captivated by the variety of memorabilia on display. Interesting talks and historical films were shown to a most attentive audience, who were also served a delicious luncheon. This was certainly the most outstanding event at the library for many a year. To add interest to the museum, Mrs Read and Mr Bill Teasdale offered to interview the old timers in the district and these tapes would be transcribed and lodged in the museum. Mrs Read would interview Mrs Monica Kemple whose father had been the first doctor at the Queen Mary Hospital.

The necessity to prop up the library finances and pay for the museum expenses resulted in fund raising, conceivably the first time in years that the library had held fund raising events for its own funds. A musical concert and an aviation symposium were held. Both events proved to be very successful and added $11,000.00 to the coffers. One hundred and twenty people attended the musical evening at a cost of $75.00 per person.

TEICHERT PRINTING PRESS

The aviation afternoon was also very well attended with curry and rice and a small bar operating.

The Chairman, Mr Peter Sternberg, moved to Harare towards the end of the year but continued as Chairman of the library, attending all the meetings. He handed over the Title Deeds of the library to Mr Bill Teasdale who lodged them in the safe at the Golden Valley Mine.

A book written on the Fitt family by Tony Fitt was purchased as the fami-

FAÇADE OF THE FITT BUILDING INCORPORATED INTO THE MUSEUM

THIS RECONSTRUCTED FRONTAGE
PART OF THE ORIGINAL FITT BUILDING
ONCE STOOD IN RHODES STREET, GATOOMA
(NOW HERBERT CHITEPO, KADOMA)
IT WAS THE FIRST TWO STORY
COMMERCIAL BUILDING ERECTED IN THE TOWN
BUILT PRIOR TO WORLD WAR 1. IT WAS CONTINUOUSLY
OCCUPIED UNTIL DEMOLISHED IN 1995.

THIS FRONTAGE, PART ORIGINAL/PART REPLICA,
WAS ERECTED UNDER THE SUPERVISION OF
MR BOB ROGERS OF KADOMA.

ly have a history with the library and it was well received.

The Saturday morning videos shows continued to be popular with the juniors and this was due to the unfailing enthusiasm of Dr Cottrell who noted that 298 shows had taken place. Letters were sent to the local schools informing them of the opening of the museum as well as other facilities available to the public. As a result of this, Mrs Read's display of "Treasures" was visited by schools as well as the general public, who enjoyed the gems of yesteryear.

An unexpected highlight of the year was that the Kadoma Library was chosen to receive a gift of books from the British Council to commemorate the approaching millennium. Mr Sternberg and Mrs Sheliegh Barton attended a function at the Council where they were presented with the gift of 250 books, to arrive over a period of 12 months: a much needed boost to the stocks.

With the advent of the millennium, the library was ending the century on an even keel. The consolidation of the previous year was continued throughout 1999 and many more books were purchased than in preceding years. This was unfortunately, not the case with suitable books for the juniors. Only two books with different and new titles had been purchased all year due to lack of supply. Many books in the booksellers were repeats of what was already on the shelves. The library was able once more, to source books from South Africa, England and the United States.

A fairy godmother had appeared in 1997 in the guise of Mrs Corley, an American benefactor. Her husband had been a mission doctor at Sanyati Mission and she had been a dedicated member – an avid reader throughout her time at the Mission. On their return to the USA, she sent regular parcels of books published by the popular authors. She continued to send these books which were often on the library shelves before they were actually in the bookshops in Zimbabwe ... a real coup for the Kadoma Library! Sadly, due to the escalating costs and high exchange rate, the overseas magazines and newspaper subscriptions had to be curtailed.

The Israeli Embassy mounted a photographic exhibition entitled, "Israel – The Holy Land" for two weeks in late October early November 1999, following a cocktail party attended by some 90 guests. Author Charles Lotter, a former schoolboy at Jameson High School and former resident of the town, presented his latest book *Echoes of an African War* to the library. Photographs and historical material continued to be donated to the library on a fairly regular basis. An important donation of chronologically bound issues of the local newspaper, *Gatooma Mail* and latterly *Kadoma Gazette* was made to the archives by Alderman Chagun Kidia. Local artists continued to display their work in the art gallery. Mrs Mary Palframan held a successful art sale and donated five per cent of sales to the library.

On the eve of the millennium after 83 years of serving the district, the library was consolidating its role as the cultural centre of the district. It also joined the 21st century by investing in a computer at a cost of Z$60,000.00. A library program (Find that Book) was sourced from Avondale Bookshop and the massive task of entering all the existing books as well as the new books began. Dr Cottrell was able to source a better school library program which was successfully installed. Previously, each new book purchased was entered into the huge non-fiction and fiction ledgers under the Dewey system. They were then also entered onto index cards. This system worked relatively well in the past but having the computer program expedited the finding of specific books and authors for the members. Using the computer necessitated the tutoring of existing staff into its uses. There was some opposition from the older staff so the task was left to computer literate volunteers. The library now had three means of cataloguing.

The most important feature of a library is its stock of books and ability to obtain the latest books, maintain their condition and discard the damaged. One of the duties of the staff has to be the repair of books which was done at that time in a quiet workroom next to the office. Here, Mr Ephraim Bongo expertly repaired books, including bookbinding and erasing of graffiti. Discarded books were still being sent to schools and the prisons. During the year in question, 390 books were put into circulation rather less than the previous year as new hardcover books were selling at Z$1,500.00 – an increase of Z$500 over 1999. Postal members dropped dramatically to nine as the costs escalated to Z$35.00 from Z$3 a couple of years back. Mr Brettell was, at the same time, ensconced in the archive room cataloguing and sorting the large amount of documents, photographs and Minute books from around the district. He also worked on a book of the *Life of John Mack*, completing it later in the year. *The Life of John Mack* was printed locally and copies were sent to all the beneficiaries of the Trust.

True to their promise, the Israeli Embassy continued to support the library. A cocktail party for 80 guests was held in the gallery where the Ambassador opened an exhibition of children's art ... the subject being "Illustrated World of the Bible". A fuel crisis had hit Zimbabwe, so people were reluctant to use their vehicles unless absolutely essential. This defined the numbers attending events and exhibitions at that time. Nevertheless, many people were able to enjoy this superb art display.

Unfortunately, there were essential staff changes. The Chief Librarian, Mrs Liz Prinsloo, had a relapse and passed away in March of 2000. After many years' service to the library, her presence, efficiency, caring and devotion to her duties at the library were sorely missed. To perpetuate her memory, the library gallery/auditorium was named the "Elizabeth Prinsloo Gallery". The Assistant Librarian, Mrs Beulah Ashby assumed the office of Chief Librarian with ease as she had worked successfully with Mrs Prinsloo for many years. Mr Alois was promoted to the main counter and Alice Kazenga became the new Children's Librarian. Alice was computer literate, so was able to assist with entering information into the computer. Mrs Stead continued as the very efficient Secretary and Mrs Dot Taylor and Mrs Debbie McDermott worked as part-time counter assistants.

The depressing economic climate in Zimbabwe in 2001 was reflected in the circumstances at the library at this time. bookshops and libraries were closing down throughout the country and no best sellers were on the shelves. If they were, they were at a cost of Z$5,100 with paper backs retailing at Z$4,000. It was almost a miracle that the library was surviving. Subsequently book purchases decreased by 63 per cent. No foreign currency was available at all, so the new book supply dried up. Yet again, subscriptions were raised as follows:

Junior member	Z$ 72-Z$ 240
Adult member	Z$300-Z$1,200
Composite members	Z$480-Z$1,800
Senior members 65+	Z$300

There was opposition to this which resulted in a drop of 120 members. The video section also suffered as there was no finance to purchase new titles. Postal members had dropped to four as the postage on a single book was Z$45. In an effort to bolster the income, the Librarian collected and sold waste paper to Marange Waste Paper. Hire fees for the auditorium were increased to Z$500 for either morning or afternoon use and Z$750 for evening use.

The Ministry of Labour in November of 2001 gazetted new wage scales for all employees. It was morally implicit, apparently, that all workers should have their wages increased by the same percentage as the lowest paid worker. In the library's case this would mean an increase of 264 per cent for each employee. At an Extraordinary Meeting of the committee, it was agreed that the library could not afford these increases. It was in the dreaded situation where income did not and had not covered expenditure for some time. Dr Cottrell suggested that he explain the situation to the staff and draw up a fair increase schedule for each employee. This would then be offered to each staff member and if they signed this agreement it would avoid redundancies.

One of the Norfolk pines, donated by Mr Harold Jackson in 1956, had grown directly across the museum roof. Mrs Stead felt that as it was bending over alarmingly and was a threat to the roof, she would find a tree cutter to give advice.

Thus ended 2001.

At the AGM in 2003, the Chairman reflected on the general conditions faced by the library in 2002 – rampant inflation, shortage of books, staffing problems and other concerns. Yet he stated that the library was amazingly resilient under the woeful conditions prevailing in Zimbabwe.

However, most catastrophic to the library was the lack of books. It had been noted with horror in 2001 the impossible increase in the cost of books but this had now reached new zeniths. The price of hardcover books had risen from Z$8,000 to Z$34,000 and that of paperbacks from Z$5,000 to Z$19,000. The committee and staff mounted a rigorous campaign appealing for books. Local residents were very supportive and the library was presented with 260 second-hand books, purchased 61 second-hand books and 30 new books This meant a reduction of books from the previous year of 78 but at least books were still getting on the shelves. Stranger still was the increase in membership by 254 members making the total membership 756. The members' reading room was proving very popular as members took advantage of the daily newspapers supplied that were retailing at Z$150 per copy.

An indication of the hard economics of life in general in Zimbabwe at that time, was the absence of exhibitions and events at the library. Nonetheless, the auditorium was hired out to the Tax Department and Mrs Read organised a display of "First Day Covers" in the exhibition room. People all over Zimbabwe were on the move, and although the library had been given fair warning, Mrs Beulah Ashby, the Chief Librarian resigned to settle with her son in South Africa and enjoy a well-earned retirement. She was sorely missed. Mrs

Colleen Barkhuizen took her place. A number of other staff left during the year. Ephraim Juju resigned due to ill-health and Alice Kazenga left abruptly in July. Charles Nykavaranda was appointed to take her position as Junior Librarian. Because the library was working on a leaner staff quota, it was decided to close the premises on Mondays and Wednesdays. This came into effect in October 2002. Likewise the children's library would be closed in the mornings during term time. For the first time in many years, the staff party was not held in deference to the paucity of funds.

Ernst and Young contacted the library early in the year informing them that there would be no pay outs from the John Mack Trust for the first part of the year as the Golden Valley Mine was also battling. Fortunately in July, they resumed monthly payments of Z$18,720 and then, quite out of the blue, Z$548,200 was received and duly invested by Dr Cottrell.

Running repairs to the building were ongoing. The mural on the wall at the children's library entrance, originally designed by Mrs Palframan and various children, was in poor shape. Mrs Rabey had attempted to organise a competition amongst the children to illustrate their favourite character from a book. If suitable they would then have been superimposed on the wall. Very disappointingly, only two were suitable, so the exercise was shelved but the two children concerned were given prizes. Eventually, when funds permitted, the said wall was painted white by a local painter.

Some years previously, 1994 to be exact, the Chairman, Mr Peter Sternberg, had emphasised that members should enjoy the golden period they were experiencing at the time as it might never come again. He was certainly prophetic in his statement as the past nine years had shown a steady deterioration in many aspects of the library. This was mainly due to the shocking economic situation in Zimbabwe. Despite unavailability of books, theft and loss of library books by members and other myriad problems, the library had survived but was conceivably entering one of the darkest periods of its existence.

Banking was becoming very expensive and Standard Bank was charging the library Z$2,000 for every third party cheque. Mrs Stead was unable to sort this problem satisfactorily so staff were to be responsible for cashing their own cheques. Dr Cottrell estimated that the income from our investments of Z$110,000.00 per month coupled with the income from subscriptions, was not sufficient for the running of the library. Therefore, subscriptions were raised considerably for a set period of six months as follows:

Adult Composite Subscription   Z$6,000
Adult Single Subscription   Z$4,000
Junior Subscription   Z$1,000

This would be reviewed every six months. There was opposition to these costs with only one adult member application after the increase. For the first time ever, it was decided to take on no more Junior Members due to non-payment of monthly subs and theft of books. Other firsts were the decision not to subscribe to Hansard which was costing Z$92,000.00 and the shelving of the yellow subscription reminder cards. Repairs to the acoustic ceiling tiles, gents' toilet door, servicing of fire extinguishers, replacement staff uniforms, picket fence, broken facia boards were progressively repaired or purchased when finance became available. Added to the stress from these problems, came the increase in theft of books. Once more, the library depended on gifts of books to fill the shelves with the occasional purchase.

Subsequently the year 2003 ended dismally.

Mr Sternberg had joined the library as a boy in 1942 and having served on the committee for an unbroken forty years, thirty-four of which had been as Chairman, tendered his resignation as Chairman of the committee at the AGM in 2004. His residency in Harare, with the necessary duties that came with it, made it virtually impossible to continue in this post but he would remain on the committee. He also announced his intention to write a history of the library and was given free range for accessing documents. Other committee members who resigned that year were emigrating to the UK viz. Mr Bill Teasdale and Mr Stanley Payne, both had been loyal members of the library for many years. Dr Howard Cottrell took over the Chair.

The new Chairman of the library, Dr Howard Cottrell was appalled by the instances of the unprecedented theft from the library. Members still left without returning their books and even denied having taken out the books and many books went missing off the shelves despite the constant vigilance of the staff. One adult and 45 juniors were blacklisted during the year for this very infringement. A female vendor was found selling at least 50 books at the market place – all owned by the library. Before she was apprehended, she hastily disappeared. The staff noted that, as people asked for specific authors listed in the computer lists, these were missing from the shelves. Of 18 Sidney Sheldon books, not one was on the shelf. The light romance section was particularly popular with thieves so this section was moved within eye-sight of the counter clerk. A certain gentleman approached the Chairman stating that he had been offered a library book for $80,000.00. The seller maintained that he had been given the book by a member of the library staff. He volunteered to take the Z$80,000.00 to the seller and would bring us details of his name and address. He was given the money and was never seen again! This was an aspect of staffing that was extremely worrying. It was so difficult to police such a large area.

Our Junior Librarian, Charles Nykavaranda announced his desire to retire through ill-health. A few months later he wrote on an official library letterhead requesting his old position back again! In the meantime, staff who took over this section found huge discrepancies in the administration of the section. Membership cards had not been issued for a long time; there were no receipts for supposed memberships. No records appeared to have been kept current. He passed away a few months' later. It was decided that his replacement, Kenny Tazviwana, would be monitored closely. The library was approached by a visitor to purchase any Rhodesiana books and other classics surplus to our needs. Mrs Barton approached a book dealer in Harare to verify prices. Library members were given the option to purchase any of these books and the remainder were offered to the visitor. Due to the prevailing suspicion of all members, there was always a modicum of doubt as to whether these were the only books taken. Mrs Barton also undertook to go through the so called "politically incorrect" books that had been taken off the shelves during the bush war and return those she felt were suitable in the new Zimbabwe.

The committee was also anxious about possible theft in the museum and Aviation Gallery. So a system of escorting visitors was introduced and a "Visitors' Book" begun. Groups were asked to make prior arrangements so that they could be accompanied by a member of staff. This system was also introduced to the large print and classic sections. All of these facilities were now under lock and key due to theft and, if they were used, the Librarian accompanied the person while they chose books or viewed the exhibits.

Despite the prevailing despondency, life went on at the library. The Gideons and the Historical Society made use of the premises. ZESA was approached to reduce the electricity tariff from commercial to normal which they agreed to do.

A notice board was placed in the foyer allowing advertisements to be mounted as well as library news. A small sum was charged for this purpose and proved very popular. The girls' toilet was found to be in

 a disgusting state, so it was kept locked and the key had to be requested. There was a significant improvement in the state of the room.

A highlight of the year was a special ceremony and cocktail party held in July 2004 to thank Mr Peter Sternberg for his years of loyal service to the library. In his honour, a plaque was placed on the Committee Room door naming this as "The Sternberg committee Room".

This was indeed a black period for the library. Only five new adult and seven new junior books were purchased. Yet again, Mrs Corley kept up a regular supply of books from the USA. Due to a steady exodus of people from the town, the library was either donated books or was able to purchase a few second-hand books. The Sternbergs, the Bartons, Dr Cottrell and Mrs Harrison also used their precious forex to purchase books. Mrs Eve, a past member, was also generous in her donation of books from South Africa. Using vendors, it was possible to maintain a reasonable supply of periodicals and newspapers. The popular *Reader's Digest* stopped coming and Mrs Stead was able to ascertain that they had closed their premises in Zimbabwe. She attempted to make contact with the magazine in the USA with little luck. Extra chairs were placed in the members' reading room due to its increased use, as newspapers and periodicals were too expensive for the man in the street to purchase personally in Zimbabwe.

Farewells were becoming too frequent. Mrs Mary Read, a member of the committee for many years, left to join her family. Mary's input into the library was enormous. She organised exhibitions, helped with the archives, displayed and labelled museum exhibits, looked after flower beds, trees and fences, books and staff. Her intelligent input at committee meetings was legendary. Her quiet, unassuming presence would be sorely missed. Another farewell was said to Lynn

Rabey a very active committee member who was leaving for England. Finances dominated each meeting during the year. Inflation was rampant. It was noted that the cost of the telephone had increased by 500 per cent. Monies invested in Intermarket were insufficient to maintain the interest being received. The minimum balance required was $20,000,000 and extra cash was not available to do this, so Dr Cottrell invested in Imara. The figures at year end were as follows:

Balance at C/A	Z$ 995,723.72
Balance at CABS C/A	Z$ 3,744,490.02
Imara Asset Investment	Z$ 6,293,139.73
Imara Asset Call Account	Z$ 52,611.92
CABS	Z$10,191,780.82

Thus the year ended with the library reasonably stable financially. Or was it?

The next years at the library were difficult. An anonymous person cheered up the staff by sending a letter stating that the library was well run and the staff very helpful! But it was still a battle obtaining new books for the library. Once again, Gayla Corley sent an amazing 96 books from America over the year. It seemed little enough, but the Sternbergs were able to take over an engraved, silver bracelet in appreciation for her ongoing support. Those bookshops still in business, demanded immediate payment for books purchased. Due to the huge increase in the price of newspapers, the committee agreed to only purchase: *The Herald*, the *South African Sunday Times*, *The Independent* and the *Weekly Telegraph*. This decision was no sooner made than prices went up by 500 per cent. Shocking as it was, another decision was made to halt the purchase of all newspapers. A library with no newspapers!

Members were also behaving badly. A total of 40 members were blacklisted and new members joined the library and one month later resigned but demanded their deposits immediately. It was agreed that deposits would only be returned after six months. However harsh this might seem, it would be an idea to mention the incredible amounts we were dealing with at that time. It was quite confusing as to where the decimal places should be for those not familiar with working with large amounts of cash. The reform campaign of *Operation Sunrise* with the motto *Zero to Hero* was launched. The old Zimbabwe bearer dollar was recalled by the Reserve Bank at the rate of 1,000 to 1, and replaced by new Bearer Cheques signed again by the Minister of Finance, Gideon Gono. The process was given short notice and with poor communications in the rural areas, many civilians were unable to convert the old notes to the new. As a matter of interest, prior to the August of 2006, the interest on the library investments was $2,419,477.25 which had to be devalued by 1,000 to 1. One can only imagine what it was like to purchase a *Fairlady* magazine for $166,500.00! Counting notes became a nightmare and note counting machines were a must. Coupled with this, was the necessity to reduce the staff from four to three and not one new member joined the library in 2006. Nonetheless, to everyone's relief, newspapers were again purchased but on a reduced selection.

Mr Ken Barton organised and paid for new shelves for the videos as well as supervising numerous repairs and maintenance in the library to light fittings and venetian blinds. Mrs Barton and Mrs Sandra Manchip updated the material in the archives as well as sorting the books on the mezzanine floor. The library was blessed with the volunteer helpers like Mrs Pam Stead, Mrs Margaret Parrock, Mrs Dorothy Taylor and Mrs Carol Lubbe. Farewells were the order of the day, unfortunately. The library was sad to lose Mrs Ina Harrison who was leaving to join her son in South Africa. Mrs Harrison had been a committee member for years and was a Library Trustee. Farewells were also said to Mr John Brettell, who had worked tirelessly on book recordings and the archives.

The library had a long history of proudly supplying the Kadoma district with a library and resource centre second to none, but the Chairman, Dr Cottrell, reported that 2007 was a difficult year. It became really difficult to ensure that the library would survive. Staffing the library became a nightmare when the Librarian, Mrs Colleen Barkhuizen left for England. Initially Mrs Wendy Crittall joined the staff but due to ill-health was forced to resign. The library was then run by Mesdames Taylor, M. Parrock, A. Oelofse, V. Cripps and various committee members, who ensured that, in the phrase heard often in World War II, "we never closed". The finances were handled, thankfully, with expertise by Mrs Aileen Burrows. Although it was a difficult situation, the input from these volunteers resulted in many changes and overall improvements to the library. Nevertheless, this effort was not sustainable for a long period as many of the volunteers had other commitments; so it was with great relief that Dr Cottrell reported the employing of a wonderful, enthusiastic, young school leaver, Carla Crous, who was waiting placement in an overseas university, as the Temporary Librarian. She tackled her job with enthusiasm, introducing new ideas and maintaining the books in impeccable order. She was able to report on the massive theft of books which was an ongoing problem at the centre. She was responsible for 471 adult members and 228 members; of these 166 adult and 121 juniors, were new members. It was interesting to note that there was a very high turnover rate in both sections. This was definitely due to the unstable financial climate.

More efficient housekeeping was introduced and Ms Crous' tight control on subscriptions helped with the financial situation. She also marketed the use of the auditorium so it was hired on numerous occasions. There was an increase in funding from the John Mack Trust that enabled the library to keep running, albeit shakily. Stevenage, Kadoma's twin city, also helped in numerous ways. Thirty-one new adult fiction and 24 second-hand books were purchased and 244 presented. A large number of those presented were, yet again, due to Mrs Gayla Corley from America. Fifty-eight books were presented. The junior section received 56 second-hand fiction and 10 non-fiction. Despite the sterling efforts of Kenny Tazviwana and Aaron Bonzo in repairing the children's books, 30 had to be discarded as being beyond repair.

The library program became obsolete and needed updating but the centre was not in a position to replace it as pound sterling was needed. The computer gave problems and was a top priority to be replaced when funds became available. All in all, it was a crisis time in the library's history and the committee was well aware that it would face challenges in the year ahead which would need to be addressed if the library was to survive.

CRISIS TIME

The writer at this time is faced with the insurmountable problem of trying to make sense of the financial chaos that shook the nation to its core in 2008 filtering in to 2009. It can only be assumed that economists have well documented this but this chapter has been written by a layman with the affairs of the library in mind and no financial or economic background. It has been noted before that inflation had gone mad and ordinary people were trying to cope with the ludicrous increase in the denomination of notes. The situation was so bad that it became necessary for the Chairman and Vice-chairman, Dr Howard Cottrell and Mrs Sheliegh Barton respectively, as well as the committee of the library to review charges, rates and salaries on a day to day basis. In December 2008, the Zimbabwe dollar halved in value every five to ten minutes. To say the situation was chaotic is putting it mildly. The banking system was at the point of collapse and the library found that after years of banking with the Standard Bank, their inefficiency and charges became more trouble than the need for the account. The CABS (Central African Building Society) account was retained.

It might be of interest to note the value of the bank notes during this period and the dates in which they were introduced.
- $50,000 (13 October 2008)
- $100,000, $500,000 and $1 million (3 November 2008)
- $10 million, $50 million and $100 million (4 December 2008)
- $200 million and $500 million (12 December 2008)
- $1 billion, $5 billion and $10 billion notes (19 December 2008)
- $20 billion and $50 billion notes (12 January 2009)

Then came the actual peak of idiocy with the introduction of the following notes in 2009: $10 trillion, $20 trillion, $50 trillion and $100 trillion (16 January 2009)

Another subject of interest was the quality of the notes. The large number of denominations issued in late-2008 as well as the suspension of paper supply by Giesecke & Devrient, affected the Reserve Bank's ability to maintain the quality of the banknotes. Giesecke &

Devrient, a Munich based firm, suspended the supply of banknote paper in response to a request from the German Government who were also calling for sanctions against the Zimbabwean Government. Notes over the years had been printed on quality paper (from the likes of the suppliers above), cotton and ordinary paper. Notes were even printed on recycled/reused paper from recalled notes. Efforts were made to retain watermarks and embedded holographic designs to prevent forgeries but were later abandoned so that many modern security features were lacking on the notes. Some of these "Bearer Cheques" even carried time limits but in some cases these were extended.

To add to the lunacy prevailing, two measures occurred. Standard Chartered Bank issued a series of emergency Bearer Cheques with Reserve Bank permission that had six months validity and the Reserve Bank issued Special Agro (Agricultural) cheques from May to July 2008. Although of a different design and with the intention for use only by farmers, these had found their way into regular use because of the parallel functions with Bearer Cheques and the exponential rise of food prices. In retrospect, how the library staff, let alone the man in the street, coped with all of this is astounding. Possibly the reason that the establishment survived is best summed up in Dr Cottrell's Chairman's report for 2008 ... "it is necessary to maintain standards and for those of us who wish to see our institutions, such as the Kadoma Library, survive and continue to provide a needed service, we have to keep the community spirit alive."

And the community came to the fore as the John Mack Trust was unable to disperse funds due to the Golden Valley Mine closure. The power bill had become unsustainable and the mine was flooding, so future funds from this source were not foreseeable at any time. Thus the public offered books and newspapers since the library could not afford to buy any books at all and gratefully accepted the 332 adult and 77 books donated as well as stationery. Digressing, the country was on its knees: Food stuffs were in short supply and supermarket shelves were bare. Those fortunate enough to have forex were able to cross the border at Botswana and South Africa to purchase essential goods.

It is almost impossible to imagine that the library continued with its mundane everyday business under these circumstances, but open it did; even to celebrate its 90th anniversary with a small celebration and the usual photoshoot per kind favour of Mr David Mason. Ms Carla Crous resigned to continue her studies. Her tenure as Assistant

Librarian had been outstanding. Her enthusiasm and new ideas were to be sadly missed. The age old problem of finding a suitable Librarian arose and the voluntary helpers stepped in before Mrs Wendy Crittall was hired again. So farewell was bade to 2008.

Man is generally optimistic by nature but 2009 and its problems were sent to try all Zimbabweans and an atmosphere of doom prevailed. This was exacerbated by the introduction on the 2nd February 2009 of the trillion dollar banknotes. It was originally envisaged that these banknotes would only remain legal tender until 30th June 2009 but all banknotes were withdrawn from circulation following the suspension of the Zimbabwe dollar on 12 April 2009. Hyperinflationary Zimbabwean banknotes (such as the $100 trillion denomination) have gained considerable interest from the numismatic community and buyers in general for its absurdity rather than the design. These notes are now being sold way in excess of their true face value.

The causes of this galloping hyperinflation were many, mostly of a political nature. The situation is succinctly explained by Joseph Noko of the Cato Institute and is well worth a read. Suffice to say that he summed it all up by writing, "Mania ... (caused by Government actions) ... brought Zimbabwe within an inch of annihilation". Finally, the government adopted the US$ as its tender and the Reserve Bank of Zimbabwe announced that balances of 0-Z$175 quadrillion would be paid a flat US$5. One can only imagine the panic this caused! On 2 February 2009, the RBZ removed 12 zeros from the currency, with 1,000,000,000,000 (third) Zimbabwe dollars being exchanged for one new (fourth) dollar. Although the dollar was abandoned on 12 April 2009, exchange rates were maintained at

intervals for some months. Therefore, the fourth dollar would be worth:
200,000,000,000,000,000,000,000,000,000,000, or
2×10^{35} first dollars if never revalued.

At the library, the situation was really critical as no monies were received, yet again, from the John Mack Trust. The library was broke! Service accounts no longer made sense, so the committee decided to pay US$5 on each account until matters settled down. Subscriptions and hiring fees had to be "dollarised" with no guidance from the banks. The problem was trying to put everything at a realistic figure; very difficult but this was managed with the usual stoicism shown by the committee. Mrs Crittall had a year of ill-health so Mrs Marie Adams' input and that of Mrs Alex Oelofse and Mrs Vanessa Crous, were of tremendous help to the centre during this difficult time. With the assistance of Mrs Aileen Burrows, reasonable sense was made of the new balances. Unfortunately, at this crucial time, Mrs Pam Stead emigrated to Australia and her expertise and enthusiasm were sorely missed. Crucial to the running of the library, were the voluntary repairs to the building by Mr Ken Barton, Mr Mike Howe and Mr Warren Oelofse and a steady supply of donated books from people leaving the town and country. Despite all of this help, the question was: Could the library survive?

Closure of the library was what faced the Chairman, committee and staff at the beginning of 2010. Even though the library did survive the economic madness of 2009, the beginning of the new decade saw the complex in real financial difficulties. The monthly income did not cover the monthly expenditure and with a shrinking membership, drastic measures were needed. Various firms and residents around town were asked to sponsor the library on a monthly basis. This was agreed to and supported by Mrs Carole Newman (a loyal and long standing member of the library), Mr Doug Palframan and Mr Mike Stravrakis. Mrs Barton targeted many embassies and non-governmental agencies for assistance but she had no response from any of them despite repeated requests. A suggestion that the public reading room, unused at the time, be hired out on a donation-type rental was agreed and, thankfully, these successful actions guaranteed a monthly income. Various minor issues dogged the library such as the demise of the computer and printer but these were overcome with the loan of computers from friends and staff. The library was, moreover, fortunate to be given many current books by well-known authors. As mentioned previously, membership was dropping particularly amongst the juniors. No particular reason could be found but it was surmised that the economic situation, TV and DVDs, computer games and tablets were possible reasons. Despite this, high standards were maintained at the centre; unique in Zimbabwe.

The financial climate was settling down and the library was able to function, albeit shakily, with the help of its sponsors and the rental of the old reading room. This income just paid the staff wages each month. The library hours were reduced so that Monday, and Wednesday afternoons it was closed and there was early closure at 12 o'clock on Saturdays.

The membership at the beginning of 2012 was:
     Adults 72   Juniors 10

What had happened to the years when the memberships numbered in the hundreds, even thousands? Could a possible reason for this lack of interest be that potential subscribers wanted to use the facilities for free? It was no consolation that libraries world-wide were experiencing the exact same difficulties, many of them "free", anyway. Video shows, that had proved so popular in previous years, were no longer supported. The advent of the Internet and Netflixs had, possibly, halted the necessity for this facility. So it was reluctantly decided to close this section.

Dejectedly, in 2011, the Chairman, Dr Cottrell noted that the library was not really being used by the people of Kadoma and district. The committee meetings were getting shorter and shorter as there were virtually no matters of importance arising, except financial matters. Even the AGMs were poorly attended, hardly making the statutory quorum. Dare it be suggested that those sections of the district population, who were enthusiastic and community minded, had left or that the current demographic makeup was of people traditionally miles apart from the concept of a library as a cultural, community centre? Whatever the reason, the Chairman said that he was determined to consider re-modelling the facility to fit in with modern standards which would mean joining the computerised generation and changing the whole concept of the library to take its place in the community.

The burning question that arose initially in 2012 was whether the library could remain open and viable. The adult membership was at an all-time low of 40+ and the Junior Section of five. Was it feasible to keep it open with such low usage? It was obviously not possible to support the library financially from these subscriptions. The rental donation from Interchem plus the ongoing generosity of the local businessmen was propping up the finances. The all-important fact was the library and its facilities were hopelessly underused and certainly did not warrant staff and committee to support this superb facility. As suggested by the Chairman in 2011, a change of usage was imperative and should be on the agenda for the future. Drastic measures were needed. History has shown that there have always been people in the Kadoma district who are passionate about the library. These people rallied around with ideas and physical help. Rotary local and in Stevenage, Hamilton King and the Alfred Beit Trust were approached to help with funds but not one of them responded. Mrs Sheliegh Barton and Mrs Sandy Manchip organised a "Save the Library" Quiz at the bowls club. This raised a small amount of funds but mainly served to highlight the dire situation at the library. An old library desk was sold and with these funds, the Venetian blinds were repaired.

Mr Barton and his helpers continued with superficial maintenance at the complex but added to the above financial distress was the condition of the library buildings in general. These were in need of painting internally and externally. The roof was leaking very badly and threatening to destroy exhibits in the museum. Once again, Mr Barton did essential repairs to the roof but it was obvious that enormous repairs were needed. Itrachem came to the fore and donated paint for a few rooms which was a much needed cosmetic exercise. Not long after this generous gesture, Intrachem moved to new premises and the hunt was on for a new tenant to replace them. To boost revenue, the children's section was portioned off and the new area created was rented out to a local lawyer. Some time prior to this, the committee had been notified that the John Mack Trust had re-opened, indicating that the Golden Valley Mine was to be resuscitated but, as this involved de-watering the mine, it would take time. The official letter from the Trust notifying the library that it would be receiving funds again was eagerly awaited but nothing arrived. An account was opened with CABS in expectation of receiving these funds and in the meantime the small amount of surplus money was used for the deposit holding.

At this stage of the library's existence, there was a small surplus of income over expenditure, which allowed the committee to purchase books in a small way; but the library still depended heavily on donations of books. The museum seemed to generate an interest amongst the general public who continued to supply many interesting exhibits which were identified and catalogued by Mrs Barton and

Mrs Manchip. There was also movement amongst the staff and committee members. Mrs Crittall resigned as Librarian and was replaced by Mrs Sharp and Mrs Sheliegh Barton resigned from the position of Vice-chairman as she was moving to Chegutu. Mr Kobus Crous replaced her as Vice-chairman. New library hours were established with the afternoon closure changed to 4.30 p.m. as there were no subscribers after that time.

Perhaps one of the saddest events of the year was the decision to cut down the remaining Norfolk pine initially known as the Jackson Pine named after the donor, Mr Harold Jackson in 1956. The tree had been a landmark in the town for 48 years but had become dangerous to the public, so tree fellers were called in and it was removed.

Donations of books continued to pour in during 2014. A total of 218 adult fiction and 137 non-fiction and 19 children's books were presented, while 218 adult books were purchased for $523.00. By careful juggling of the small, at times, surplus and generous donations, the library was able to function for the first part of the year. Rental donations brought in $8,100.00 and subscriptions $1,744.00. These figures serve to show how few members were paid up. Hire of the auditorium brought in only $80.00 and wages continued to be the greatest expense at $6,850.00. But as it had done for years, the library operated.

In the middle of 2014, the Chairman was delighted to receive a letter from the John Mack Trust informing him that the library would be receiving a one off payment of $10,000. In following the wishes of the Trust, it was decided to use this money for the urgently required maintenance at the library. The items urgently in need of repair were the roof and facia boards damaged over the years by the weather. A realistic quote was obtained and authorised and, after a few problems, the work was completed satisfactorily. This injection of capital served to rejuvenate enthusiasm for the day to day running of the complex. Mesdames Barton and Manchip with the help of the Librarian updated the museum artefacts. Animal trophies donated by Mrs Alison Peters were affixed throughout the library and became a real point of interest to the children. Mrs Tanya Barnard offered to restructure the children's library and was invited to join the committee. Sir John Kennedy School approached the Librarian with a request for a block booking for the children which was granted and it was a pleasure to see children enthusiastically reading the books once again. A local artist hired the auditorium and held a successful exhibition of his artwork. For the first time in its history, the library was passed a fake $100.00 bill. The library eventually entered the 21st century by updating computer equipment and accessing the Internet. Such was the importance of the bequest of a man all those years ago that an institute, about to fold and crumble, was able to revive.

Mr and Mrs Barton were unable to commit to the library from their new home in Chegutu, and regretfully resigned at the end of the year. The Chairman thanked them for their years of dedication to the library at a small evening gathering held in the display room. It seems that the history of the library is almost becoming a tale of economic woes and not the tale of an institute central to cultural and community life.

Indeed, 2015 was ushered in with more problems. The roof leaks, previously thought to have been sorted, were once again an issue. Added to this, the tenant in the old children's library complained that the vinyl floor tiles were lifting and breaking. Thus began a period of repairs and replacements to the existing tiles and roof leaks. Electrical consumption had risen substantially and as the meter was shared with the tenants, it was proposed to install separate meters for each section. One tenant was evicted for non-payment of rent in the sum of $900.00. However, this was only after assistance from lawyers, whose costs were iniquitous.

Mrs Barnard resigned from the committee and Mrs Sigrid Stone joined with Mrs Maggie Britz asked and agreeing to be the Financial Advisor. Aaron Bonzo continued as general factotum and was definitely appreciated for being responsible for the smooth day to day cleaning and sorting of books.

A decidedly unpleasant situation arose. The Chairman had to ask the Librarian to leave her position after major discrepancies in her work and library finances were revealed. Mrs Marie Adams agreed to temporarily fill in running the library until a new Librarian could be found. Fortunately, Mrs Crittall was available and was, once more, appointed as Librarian. Mrs Britz, Mrs Adams and Mrs Crittall set to work sorting out the finances which were quite chaotic. It was also established that during the tenure of the previous Librarian, the catalogue ledgers were missing and the computer program was out of date. To ensure continuity of records, an external hard drive was purchased as well as an inverter. For the first time, the library used an e-mail address. Mrs Britz was then asked to become a member of the committee. Fortunately, a new tenant, a lawyer, was found to hire the old public reading room.

Lady Tait School, following in the footsteps of Sir John Kennedy School, requested and were given a block subscription. The children were now using the facilities enthusiastically.

With further funds from the John Mack Trust and with the permission of the Trustees, minor repairs and replacements were done. The monies received from the Trust took the pressure off the immediate financial concerns but 2016 heralded a new apprehension. Zimbabwe was alarmingly short of actual cash. The country owed millions to the IMF and World Bank, the immediate amount of which was paid somehow. The people of Zimbabwe were once more faced with an issue of Bond notes at the end of October 2016. These came in $2 and $5 notes as well as a $1 Bond coin and were supposed to have the same exchange rate as the US$ i.e. 1:1. The shortage of cash necessitated the staff being required to open bank accounts or Eco cash accounts as the only way to "have" money was in an account and payments were made by using cards or transferring money from one account to another. These situations have been well documented elsewhere, but, suffice to say, the strain on the populace was shocking. Yet again the library managed to survive. This was due mainly to the local community who assisted in many ways during the year. Mr John Kinnaird repaired the fountain, which was immediately vandalised; Mr Charles Robertson donated aggregate for library use; a water tank was installed to alleviate the water shortage from municipal supplies and Mr Gavin Otter's help in this respect was invaluable. Repairs and replacements were ongoing and a small book supply was maintained for our small number of subscribers.

The staff remains at two: the Librarian, Mrs Wendy Crittall and Mr Aaron Bongo. Mrs Margaret Parrock joined the committee after many years as a friend of the library.

A NEW DAWN?

The 100 year anniversary year has dawned at last ... 2017. At the date of writing this in June 2017, we have not yet reached November which is the actual 100th anniversary.

The library has modernised indeed by changing a portion of the members' reading room into a public Internet facility. Six computers have been purchased and the system installed. It is hoped that this facility will be of enormous benefit to the public of Kadoma who will have 21st century facilities to hand. US$215.00 has been spent on books to date and the John Mack Trust revenue is standing at $13,909.79 at the time of writing, so dare we think a new dawn is here?

Cast your minds back to the beginning of this tale where enthusiasm abounds.

By 1917 Gatooma had developed into a town, and was awarded municipal status that same year. The first Mayor to be elected was none other than the previously mentioned George Septimus Fitt, a major supporter of the movement to establish a library in the town. The clamour for a decently sized library had in the meanwhile increased, and so it was that a public meeting of likely subscribers to a library was arranged, and was held in the lounge of Specks Hotel on Friday 30th November 1917. Twenty people turned up, including one lady, and Mr Alex R. Garrett took the Chair. Mr Garrett and Mr E. R. Blackwell outlined their plans to form a public library, and these were found acceptable. Mr R. W. Pringle proposed that the library be named "The Gatooma & District Public Library" after Mr Calder had suggested that the word "District" be added to the name. Five persons were elected to the first committee, namely Messrs. Garrett, Thornton, Pringle, the Revd Green and Miss Phelps. It was also proposed and seconded that Mr E. R. Blackwell be elected Hon. Treasurer. The motion that a room be hired for one pound a month to house the books was carried. **And so ended a meeting which would have far ranging consequences over the years to come ...**

And we can rightly say that the last few words of that paragraph are so true. The consequences of that meeting have resulted in a fantastic, modern, library. Loved and used over the past 100 years by young and old, rich and poor and surviving many disasters and circumstances, the present day library soldiers on with day to day housekeeping and maintenance; continuing in much the same way it did in 1917, with much the same objects ... a fantastic benefit for the people of Kadoma and District. However, with only 44 adult members (only seven more than the original members 100 years ago) and two junior members, this question arises:

Can the library survive for another 100 years?

Only history will tell ...

ANNIVERSARIES

LIBRARY CHAIRMEN

OLGA DE MEILLION

ROBERT STERNBERG

PETER STERNBERG

LIBRARIANS

KAY STRICKLAND

DORIS REINER

ELIZABETH (LIZ)
PRINSLOO

BULEAH ASHBY

ACKNOWLEDGEMENTS

My beloved husband Peter Sternberg, whose devoted interest in the Gatooma/Kadoma Library made a major contribution to it being recognized as a leading institution of its kind in the country.

My thanks go to Sheliegh Barton, our very close friend, who kindly agreed to complete this book after the untimely passing of Peter. It was Peter's desire that this book be ready in time to celebrate the 100th year anniversary of the Kadoma Library. She has helped to make this possible.

Thank you, too, to all those wonderful people, too many to name, who, over the years have contributed in one way or another to the success of the library.

Hermoine Sternberg

www.ingramcontent.com/pod-product-compliance
Lightning Source LLC
Chambersburg PA
CBHW071730090426
42738CB00011B/2449